EXERCISE 13.8

Y0-BPX-566

ACCOUNT NAME	DEBIT	CREDIT

PROBLEM 13.1A or 13.1B

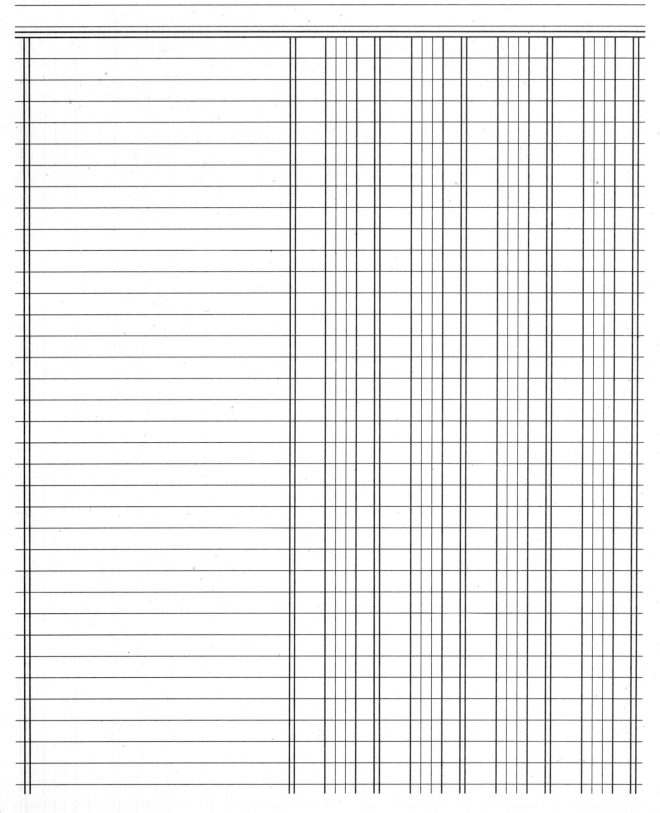

(continued)

Study Guide & Working Papers
for use with

College Accounting

CHAPTERS 1–13
ELEVENTH EDITION

John Ellis Price

M. David Haddock

Horace R. Brock

McGraw-Hill
Irwin

Boston   Burr Ridge, IL   Dubuque, IA   Madison, WI   New York   San Francisco   St. Louis
Bangkok   Bogotá   Caracas   Kuala Lumpur   Lisbon   London   Madrid   Mexico City
Milan   Montreal   New Delhi   Santiago   Seoul   Singapore   Sydney   Taipei   Toronto

Study Guide & Working Papers for use with
COLLEGE ACCOUNTING, Eleventh Edition
Chapters 1–13
John Ellis Price, M. David Haddock, Jr., and Horace R. Brock

Published by McGraw-Hill/Irwin, a business unit of The McGraw-Hill Companies, Inc., 1221
Avenue of the Americas, New York, NY 10020. Copyright © 2007 by The McGraw-Hill
Companies, Inc.
All rights reserved.

2 3 4 5 6 7 8 9 0 QPD/QPD 0 9 8 7

ISBN: 978-0-07-303059-3 (chapters 1–32)
MHID: 0-07-303059-7 (chapters 1–32)
ISBN: 978-0-07-303058-6 (chapters 14–25)
MHID: 0-07-303058-9 (chapters 14–25)
ISBN: 978-0-07-320348-5 (chapters 1–13)
MHID: 0-07-320348-3 (chapters 1–13)

www.mhhe.com

Contents

CHAPTER 1

Accounting: The Language of Business

STUDY GUIDE

Understanding the Chapter

Objectives

1. Define accounting. **2.** Identify and discuss career opportunities in accounting. **3.** Identify the users of financial information. **4.** Compare and contrast the three types of business entities. **5.** Describe the process used to develop generally accepted accounting principles. **6.** Define the accounting terms new to this chapter.

Reading Assignment

Read Chapter 1 in the textbook. Complete the textbook Section Self Review as you finish reading each section of the chapter, and the Comprehensive Self Review at the end of the chapter. Refer to the Chapter 1 Glossary or to the Glossary at the end of the book to find definitions for terms that are not familiar to you.

Activities

❑ **Thinking Critically**

Answer the *Thinking Critically* questions for Yahoo and Managerial Implications.

❑ **Discussion Questions**

Answer each assigned discussion question in Chapter 1.

❑ **Critical Thinking Problem**

Complete the critical thinking problem as assigned.

❑ **Business Connections**

Complete the Business Connections activities as assigned to gain a deeper understanding of Chapter 1 concepts.

Practice Tests

Complete the Practice Tests, which cover the main points in your reading assignment. Compare your answers with those in the Practice Test Answer Key for Chapter 1 at the end of this chapter. If you have answered any questions incorrectly, review the related section of the text.

Part A True-False *For each of the following statements, circle T in the answer column if the answer is true or F if the answer is false.*

T   F   **1.** Passing a test called the Uniform CPA Examination is required for one to become a certified public accountant.

T   F   **2.** The Securities and Exchange Commission has a great deal of power to dictate accounting methods used by companies whose stock is traded on the stock exchanges.

T   F   **3.** The Securities and Exchange Commission often relies on pronouncements of the Financial Accounting Standards Board.

T   F   **4.** The Financial Accounting Standards Board issues income tax rules.

T   F   **5.** Because of the separate entity assumption, the personal financial activities of the owner of a sole proprietorship are combined with the financial affairs of his or her business in the accounting records of the business.

T   F   **6.** All accounting principles are established by law.

T   F   **7.** Because of the difference in the structures of the three types of business entities, certain aspects of their financial affairs are accounted for in different ways.

T   F   **8.** A sole proprietorship is a form of business entity owned by two or more people.

T   F   **9.** There is little difference between a corporation and other forms of business entities.

T   F   **10.** Shares of stock represent ownership in a corporation.

T   F   **11.** Employees should have no particular interest in the financial information about the business for which they work.

T   F   **12.** The American Institute of Certified Public Accountants is a governmental agency.

T   F   **13.** In a large company, the auditing process is completed by bookkeepers.

Part B Completion   *In the answer column, supply the missing word or words needed to complete each of the following statements.*

_____ 1. The _____ and other tax authorities are interested in financial information about a firm.

_____ 2. Corporate owners are called _____.

_____ 3. Ownership in a corporation is evidenced by _____.

_____ 4. The three major types of business entities are sole proprietorships, corporations, and _____.

_____ 5. An economic entity is an organization whose major purpose is to produce a profit, whereas a(n) _____ is a nonprofit organization.

_____ 6. The accounting process involves _____, summarizing, interpreting, and communicating financial information about an economic or social entity.

_____ 7. Many people call accounting the _____.

_____ 8. Periodic reports prepared from accounting records are called _____.

_____ 9. _____ is the study of accounting principles used by different countries.

_____ 10. The IRS and the _____ have large numbers of accountants on their staff and use them to uncover possible violations of the law.

_____ 11. Major areas of accounting are public accounting, managerial accounting, and _____.

_____ 12. The _____ is an organization of accounting educators.

_____ 13. The _____ is a national association of professional accountants.

_____ 14. _____ are developed by the Financial Accounting Standards Board.

_____ 15. The _____ was created to review and oversee the accounting methods of publicly owned corporations.

WORKING PAPERS

CHAPTER 1 CRITICAL THINKING PROBLEM

_____

_____

_____

_____

_____

_____

_____

_____

_____

_____

_____

_____

_____

_____

_____

_____

_____

_____

_____

_____

_____

_____

_____

_____

_____

Chapter 1 Practice Test Answer Key

Part A True-False	Part B Completion
1. T	1. IRS
2. T	2. stockholders or shareholders
3. T	3. shares of stock
4. F	4. partnerships
5. F	5. social entity
6. F	6. recording, classifying
7. T	7. language of business
8. F	8. financial statements
9. F	9. International accounting
10. T	10. FBI
11. F	11. government accounting
12. F	12. AAA
13. F	13. AICPA
	14. Generally accepted accounting principles
	15. SEC

CHAPTER 2 Analyzing Business Transactions

STUDY GUIDE

Understanding the Chapter

Objectives	**1.** Record in equation form the financial effects of a business transaction. **2.** Define, identify, and understand the relationship between asset, liability, and owner's equity accounts. **3.** Analyze the effects of business transactions on a firm's assets, liabilities, and owner's equity and record these effects in accounting equation form. **4.** Prepare an income statement. **5.** Prepare a statement of owner's equity and a balance sheet **6.** Define the accounting terms new to this chapter.
Reading Assignment	Read Chapter 2 in the textbook. Complete the textbook Section Self Review as you finish reading each section of the chapter, and the Comprehensive Self Review at the end of the chapter. Refer to the Chapter 2 Glossary or to the Glossary at the end of the book to find definitions for terms that are not familiar to you.

Activities

❏ **Thinking Critically**	Answer the *Thinking Critically* questions for Southwest Airlines, Accounting on the Job, and Managerial Implications.
❏ **Internet Application**	Complete the activity for Accounting on the Job.
❏ **Discussion Questions**	Answer each assigned discussion question in Chapter 2.
❏ **Exercises**	Complete each assigned exercise in Chapter 2. Use the forms provided in this SGWP. The objectives covered by an exercise are given after the exercise number. If you need help with an exercise, review the portion of the chapter related to the objective(s) covered.
❏ **Problems A/B**	Complete each assigned problem in Chapter 2. Use the forms provided in this SGWP. The objectives covered by a problem are given after the problem number. If you need help with a problem, review the portion of the chapter related to the objective(s) covered.
❏ **Challenge Problem**	Complete the challenge problem as assigned. Use the forms provided in this SGWP.
❏ **Critical Thinking Problem**	Complete the critical thinking problem as assigned. Use the forms provided in this SGWP.
❏ **Business Connections**	Complete the Business Connections activities as assigned to gain a deeper understanding of Chapter 2 concepts.

Practice Tests

Complete the Practice Tests, which cover the main points in your reading assignment. Compare your answers with those in the Practice Test Answer Key for Chapter 2 at the end of this chapter. If you have answered any questions incorrectly, review the related section of the text.

Part A True-False *For each of the following statements, circle T in the answer column if the answer is true or F if the answer is false.*

T   F   **1.** When equipment is purchased for cash, there is no change in the total value of the firm's property.

T   F   **2.** The balance sheet is prepared at the end of the accounting period to show the results of operations.

T   F   **3.** A net loss results if total expenses exceed total revenue.

T   F   **4.** Profit and loss statement is another name for the income statement.

T   F   **5.** The balance sheet shows the financial position of a business on a specific date.

T   F   **6.** The net income or net loss for the period is shown in the Assets section of the balance sheet.

T   F   **7.** The net income or net loss for the period is shown on both the income statement and the statement of owner's equity.

T   F   **8.** The collection of cash from accounts receivable increases owner's equity.

T   F   **9.** Expenses decrease owner's equity.

T   F   **10.** Revenue decreases owner's equity.

Part B Matching *For each numbered item, choose the matching term from the box and write the identifying letter in the answer column.*

_____   **1.** Amounts owed by charge account customers

_____   **2.** Amount remaining when total revenue is more than total expenses

_____   **3.** Those to whom money is owed

_____   **4.** Owner's financial interest in the business

_____   **5.** Property owned by a business

_____   **6.** A business obligation or debt

_____   **7.** An expression of the relationship in which assets equal liabilities plus owner's equity

_____   **8.** Inflows of money or other assets resulting from sales of goods or service

a. Accounts Receivable

b. Assets

c. Creditors

d. Revenue

e. Owner's equity

f. Liability

g. Net income

h. Fundamental accounting equation

Part C Completion

In the answer column, supply the missing word or words needed to complete each of the following statements.

_____ 1. Accountants must _____ each business transaction before they can intelligently record, report, and interpret it.

_____ 2. The purchase of new equipment on account creates a debt that is called a(n) _____.

_____ 3. When property values and financial interest increase or decrease, the sum of the items on both sides of the equation always remains _____.

_____ 4. The basic reason for starting a business is the possibility of making a _____.

_____ 5. Accounts receivable result when goods are sold or services are performed on _____.

_____ 6. When expenses are paid, the owner's equity is _____.

_____ 7. Regardless of the number and variety of transactions, liabilities plus owner's equity always equal _____.

_____ 8. When supplies are first purchased for use in operations, they are considered a type of _____.

Demonstration Problem

The account balances for Kawonza Carter, CPA, for the month of January 2007 are shown below in random order.

Rent Expense	$ 8,000	Advertising Expense	$ 5,000
Fees Earned	138,240	Office Equipment	51,120
Accounts Payable	29,824	K. Carter, Drawing	15,156
Salaries Expense	23,780	Accounts Receivable	29,800
Cash	182,276	K. Carter, Capital 1/1	?

Instructions

1. Determine the balance for **Kawonza Carter, Capital,** on January 1, 2007.
2. Prepare an income statement, a statement of owner's equity, and a balance sheet as of January 31, 2007.

SOLUTION

Determine the balance for Kawonza Carter, Capital, on January 1, 2007.
Let Kawonza Carter, Capital = X. Solving for X:

		Assets			=	Liabilities	+		Owner's Equity					
Cash	+	Accts. Rec.	+	Office Equip.	=	Accounts Pay.	+	K. Carter, Capital	− Drawing	+ Revenue	− Expenses

Cash	+	Accts. Rec.	+	Office Equip.	=	Accounts Pay.	+	K. Carter, Capital	−	Drawing	+	Revenue	−	Expenses
182,276	+	29,800	+	51,120	=	29,824	+	X	−	15,156	+	138,240	−	36,780
				263,196	=	116,128	+	X						
		263,196	−	116,128	=	X								
				147,068	=	X								

Kawonza Carter, Capital, January 1, 2007 = **$147,068**

Total Expenses:

Rent Expense	$ 8,000
Salaries Expense	23,780
Advertising Expense	5,000
	$36,780

Kawonza Carter, CPA

Income Statement

Month Ended January 31, 2007

Revenue		
Fees Earned		138 2 4 0 00
Expenses		
Rent Expense	8 0 0 0 00	
Salaries Expense	23 7 8 0 00	
Advertising Expense	5 0 0 0 00	
Total Expenses		36 7 8 0 00
Net Income		101 4 6 0 00

Kawonza Carter, CPA

Statement of Owner's Equity

Month Ended January 31, 2007

Kawonza Carter, Capital, January 1, 2007		147 0 6 8 00
Net Income	101 4 6 0 00	
Less Withdrawals	15 1 5 6 00	
Increase in Capital		86 3 0 4 00
Kawonza Carter, Capital, January 31, 2007		233 3 7 2 00

SOLUTION (continued)

Kawonza Carter, CPA
Balance Sheet
January 31, 2007

Assets						Liabilities					
Cash	182	2	7	6	00	Accounts Payable	29	8	2	4	00
Accounts Receivable	29	8	0	0	00	Owner's Equity					
Office Equipment	51	1	2	0	00	Kawonza Carter, Capital	233	3	7	2	00
Total Assets	263	1	9	6	00	Total Liabilities and Owner's Equity	263	1	9	6	00

WORKING PAPERS

Name _____

EXERCISE 2.1

1. _____
2. _____
3. _____
4. _____
5. _____

EXERCISE 2.2

Assets _____

Liabilities _____

Owner's Equity _____

EXERCISE 2.3

	Assets	=	Liabilities	+	Owner's Equity
1.	_____	=	_____	+	_____
2.	_____	=	_____	+	_____
3.	_____	=	_____	+	_____
4.	_____	=	_____	+	_____
5.	_____	=	_____	+	_____

EXERCISE 2.4

Transaction	Assets	=	Liabilities	+	Owner's Equity
1.	_____ + _____	=	_____	+	_____ + _____
2.	_____	=	_____	+	_____
3.	_____	=	_____	+	_____
4.	_____	=	_____	+	_____
5.	_____	=	_____	+	_____
6.	_____	=	_____	+	_____
7.	_____	=	_____	+	_____
8.	_____	=	_____	+	_____
9.	_____	=	_____	+	_____
10.	_____	=	_____	+	_____

EXERCISE 2.5

	Assets			= Liabilities	+	Owner's Equity		
Cash	+ Accounts Receivable	+ Equipment	=	Accounts Payable	+ Inez Owens Capital	+ Revenue	− Expenses

1. _____
2. _____
3. _____
4. _____
5. _____
6. _____
7. _____
8. _____

Totals _____ + _____ + _____ = _____ + _____ − _____

EXERCISE 2.6

1. _____
2. _____
3. _____
4. _____
5. _____
6. _____
7. _____

EXERCISE 2.7

_____

<u>Revenue</u>

_____

<u>Expenses</u>

_____
_____
_____
_____
_____
_____
_____

EXERCISE 2.8

Revenue

Expenses

EXERCISE 2.9

EXERCISE 2.10

PROBLEM 2.1A or 2.1B

	Cash	+	Accounts Receivable	+	Supplies	+	Equipment	=	Accounts Payable	+	Owner's Capital
					Assets			=	Liabilities	+	Owner's Equity
1.											
2.											
3.											
4.											
5.											
6.											
7.											
8.											
9.											
10.											
11.											
Totals		+		+		+		=		+	
								=			

Analyze: _____

_____

PROBLEM 2.2A or 2.2B

		Assets		= Liabilities +		Owner's Equity		
	Cash	+ Accounts Receivable +	+ _____	= Accounts Payable	+ Capital	+ Revenue	− Expenses
Beginning Balances	_____ +	_____ +	_____ +	= _____	+ _____	+ _____	− _____
1.	_____	_____	_____				
New Balances	_____ +	_____ +	_____ +	= _____	+ _____	+ _____	− _____
2.	_____	_____	_____				
New Balances	_____ +	_____ +	_____ +	= _____	+ _____	+ _____	− _____
3.	_____	_____	_____				
New Balances	_____ +	_____ +	_____ +	= _____	+ _____	+ _____	− _____
4.	_____	_____	_____				
New Balances	_____ +	_____ +	_____ +	= _____	+ _____	+ _____	− _____
5.	_____	_____	_____				
New Balances	_____ +	_____ +	_____ +	= _____	+ _____	+ _____	− _____
6.	_____	_____	_____				
New Balances	_____ +	_____ +	_____ +	= _____	+ _____	+ _____	− _____
7.	_____	_____	_____				
New Balances	_____ +	_____ +	_____ +	= _____	+ _____	+ _____	− _____
8.	_____	_____	_____				
New Balances	_____ +	_____ +	_____ +	= _____	+ _____	+ _____	− _____
9.	_____	_____	_____				
New Balances	_____ +	_____ +	_____ +	= _____	+ _____	+ _____	− _____
10.	_____	_____	_____				
New Balances	_____ +	_____ +	_____ +	= _____	+ _____	+ _____	− _____
				=			

Analyze: _____

_____

PROBLEM 2.3A or 2.3B

_____

_____

_____

Analyze: _____

_____

PROBLEM 2.4A or 2.4B

_____

_____

PROBLEM 2.4A or 2.4B (continued)

CHAPTER 2 CHALLENGE PROBLEM

Determine the balance for **French Taylor, Capital**, April 1, 2007.

			=	Liabilities +			Owner's Equity			
		Assets								
		Accounts			Accounts	French Taylor	French Taylor			
Cash	+ Receivable	+ Machinery	=	Payable	+ Capital	− Drawing	+ Revenue	− Expenses		
$6,500	+ $2,800	+ $8,500	=	$3,200	+ ?	− $1,200	+ $9,500	− $5,000		

Let French Taylor, Capital = X.

Solving for X:

French Taylor, Capital, April 1, 2007, = _____

Advertising Expense	$ 900
Maintenance Expense	1,100
Salaries Expense	3,000
Total Expenses	=======

CHAPTER 2 CHALLENGE PROBLEM (continued)

Analyze: _____

CHAPTER 2 CRITICAL THINKING PROBLEM

Chapter 2 Practice Test Answer Key

Part A True-False		Part B Matching		Part C Completion	
1. T	6. F	1. a	5. b	1. analyze	5. credit or on account
2. F	7. T	2. g	6. f	2. accounts payable or liability	6. reduced or decreased
3. T	8. F	3. c	7. h	3. equal	7. assets
4. T	9. T	4. e	8. d	4. profit	8. asset or property
5. T	10. F				

20 ■ Chapter 2

Copyright © 2007 The McGraw-Hill Companies, Inc. All rights reserved.

CHAPTER 3

Analyzing Business Transactions Using T Accounts

STUDY GUIDE

Understanding the Chapter

Objectives

1. Set up T accounts for assets, liabilities, and owner's equity. **2.** Analyze business transactions and enter them in the accounts. **3.** Determine the balance of an account. **4.** Set up T accounts for revenue and expenses. **5.** Prepare a trial balance from T accounts. **6.** Prepare an income statement, a statement of owner's equity, and a balance sheet. **7.** Develop a chart of accounts. **8.** Define the accounting terms new to this chapter.

Reading Assignment

Read Chapter 3 in the textbook. Complete the textbook Section Self Review as you finish reading each section of the chapter, and the Comprehensive Self Review at the end of the chapter. Refer to the Chapter 3 Glossary or to the Glossary at the end of the book to find definitions for terms that are not familiar to you.

Activities

❑ **Thinking Critically**

Answer the *Thinking Critically* questions for Johnson & Johnson, Computers in Accounting, and Managerial Implications.

❑ **Internet Application**

Complete the activity for Computers in Accounting.

❑ **Discussion Questions**

Answer each assigned discussion question in Chapter 3.

❑ **Exercises**

Complete each assigned exercise in Chapter 3. Use the forms provided in this SGWP. The objectives covered by an exercise are given after the exercise number. If you need help with an exercise, review the portion of the chapter related to the objective(s) covered.

❑ **Problems A/B**

Complete each assigned problem in Chapter 3. Use the forms provided in this SGWP. The objectives covered by a problem are given after the problem number. If you need help with a problem, review the portion of the chapter related to the objective(s) covered.

❑ **Challenge Problem**

Complete the challenge problem as assigned. Use the forms provided in this SGWP.

❑ **Critical Thinking Problem**

Complete the critical thinking problem as assigned. Use the forms provided in this SGWP.

❑ **Business Connections**

Complete the Business Connections activities as assigned to gain a deeper understanding of Chapter 3 concepts.

Practice Tests

Complete the Practice Tests, which cover the main points in your reading assignment. Compare your answers with those in the Practice Test Answer Key for Chapter 3 at the end of this chapter. If you have answered any questions incorrectly, review the related section of the text.

Part A True-False *For each of the following statements, circle T in the answer column if the answer is true or F if the answer is false.*

T F **1.** The **Accounts Payable** account is decreased by a debit entry.

T F **2.** Increases in expense accounts are recorded by credit entries.

T F **3.** Accountants keep a separate record for each asset, liability, and owner's equity item.

T F **4.** The T account allows increases and decreases to be separated and recorded on different sides.

T F **5.** Increases in assets are recorded on the debit side of an account.

T F **6.** Decreases in assets are recorded on the left side of an account.

T F **7.** The owner's beginning investment is entered as a debit in the owner's capital account.

T F **8.** Increases in liabilities are recorded on the debit side of an account.

T F **9.** A cash payment by a business is recorded as a debit entry in the **Cash** account.

T F **10.** Decreases in liabilities are credited to the liability account.

T F **11.** An increase in the owner's investment is recorded by crediting the owner's capital account.

T F **12.** Revenue accounts are increased by credits.

T F **13.** An entry on the left side of any account is called a debit.

T F **14.** A reduction in the equity of the owners is recorded by making a debit entry in the **Owner's Capital** account.

T F **15.** The receipt of cash is recorded by a debit entry to the **Cash** account.

Part B Matching   *For each numbered item, choose the matching item from the box and write the identifying letter in the answer column.*

_____   1. An operating cost that decreases owner's equity.

_____   2. The system of accounting that requires equality of the entries on each side of the equation.

_____   3. Accounts whose balances are carried forward to start a new period.

_____   4. An entry on the left side of an account.

_____   5. A system for arranging accounts in logical order.

_____   6. An entry on the right side of an account.

_____   7. Accounts whose balances are transferred to a summary account at the end of the accounting period.

_____   8. A subdivision of owner's equity that is used to record various types of income of a business.

_____   9. A separate written record that is kept for each asset, liability, and owner's equity item.

a. Account
b. Double-entry system
c. Credit
d. Permanent accounts
e. Temporary accounts
f. Expense
g. Revenue
h. Chart of accounts
i. Debit

Part C Completion   *In the answer column, supply the missing word or words needed to complete each of the following statements.*

_____   1. The _____ of an account is where increases in the account are recorded and where the balance is recorded.

_____   2. The _____ is a statement prepared to test the accuracy of the figures recorded in the accounts.

_____   3. A(n) _____ is an error where the decimal point is misplaced.

_____   4. A(n) _____ is an error where the digits of a number are switched.

_____   5. A(n) _____ is the total of several entries on either side of an account that is entered in small pencil.

Demonstration Problem

Adiam Ghirmai is an investment broker who operates her own business, Ghirmai Investment Counseling.

Instructions

1. Analyze the transactions for the month of January 2007, and record each in the appropriate T accounts. Use plus and minus signs to show increases and decreases. Identify each entry in the T accounts by writing the number of the transaction next to the entry.

2. Determine the balance for each T account. Prepare a trial balance.

Transactions

1. Adiam Ghirmai invested $25,000 in cash to start the business.

2. Ghirmai Investment Counseling purchased office furniture for $4,500 on account.

3. Paid $1,500 for one month's rent.

4. Sold an investment portfolio to the Inez Family and received fees of $25,000.

5. Purchased a computer for $2,000, paying $1,000 in cash and putting the balance on account for 60 days.

6. Paid $4,200 for employee salaries.

7. Purchased office equipment for $3,750 with credit terms of 60 days.

8. Sold an investment portfolio to the Reed Family and will receive commission fees of $10,500 in 30 days.

9. Issued a check for $1,875 for partial payment of the amount for office equipment.

10. Adiam Ghirmai withdrew $2,500 in cash for personal use.

11. Issued a check for $520 to pay the utility bill.

SOLUTION

	Cash					Accounts Receivable				Office Furniture	
(1)	+ 25,000	(3)	− 1,500		(8)	+ 10,500			(2)	+ 4,500	
(4)	+ 25,000	(5)	− 1,000								
		(6)	− 4,200								
		(9)	− 1,875			**Office Equipment**				**Accounts Payable**	
	50,000	(10)	− 2,500		(5)	+ 2,000			(9)	− 1,875	(2) + 4,500
		(11)	− 520		(7)	+ 3,750					(5) + 1,000
Bal.	38,405		11,595		Bal.	5,750					(7) + 3,750
											Bal. 7,375

	Adiam Ghirmai, Capital			Adiam Ghirmai, Drawing			Fees Income	
		(1) + 25,000	(10)	+ 2,500			(4)	+ 25,000
							(8)	+ 10,500
							Bal.	35,500

	Rent Expense			Salaries Expense			Utilities Expense	
(3)	+ 1,500		(6)	+ 4,200		(11)	+ 520	

SOLUTION (continued)

Ghirmai Investment Counseling

Trial Balance

January 31, 2007

ACCOUNT NAME	DEBIT	CREDIT
Cash	38 4 0 5 00	
Accounts Receivable	10 5 0 0 00	
Office Furniture	4 5 0 0 00	
Office Equipment	5 7 5 0 00	
Accounts Payable		7 3 7 5 00
Adiam Ghirmai, Capital		25 0 0 0 00
Adiam Ghirmai, Drawing	2 5 0 0 00	
Fees Income		35 5 0 0 00
Rent Expense	1 5 0 0 00	
Salaries Expense	4 2 0 0 00	
Utilities Expense	5 2 0 00	
Totals	67 8 7 5 00	67 8 7 5 00

WORKING PAPERS

Name _____

EXERCISE 3.1

EXERCISE 3.2

EXERCISE 3.3

1. _____
2. _____
3. _____
4. _____
5. _____

EXERCISE 3.4

1. _____   5. _____

2. _____   6. _____

3. _____   7. _____

4. _____   8. _____

EXERCISE 3.5

_____   _____

_____   _____

_____   _____

_____   _____

_____   _____

EXERCISE 3.6

_____

_____

ACCOUNT NAME	DEBIT	CREDIT

EXERCISE 3.6 (continued)

EXERCISE 3.7

EXERCISE 3.7 (continued)

EXERCISE 3.8

PROBLEM 3.1A or 3.1B

1. _____|_____   _____|_____

2. _____|_____   _____|_____

3. _____|_____   _____|_____

4. _____|_____   _____|_____

5. _____|_____   _____|_____

6. _____|_____   _____|_____

7. _____|_____   _____|_____

8. _____|_____   _____|_____

Analyze: _____

_____

PROBLEM 3.2A or 3.2B

1. _____|_____   _____|_____

2. _____|_____   _____|_____

3. _____|_____   _____|_____

4. _____|_____   _____|_____

5. _____|_____   _____|_____

6. _____|_____   _____|_____

7. _____|_____   _____|_____

8. _____|_____   _____|_____

Analyze: _____

_____

PROBLEM 3.3A or 3.3B

1. _____|_____   _____|_____

2. _____|_____   _____|_____

3. _____|_____   _____|_____

4. _____|_____   _____|_____

5. _____|_____   _____|_____

6. _____|_____   _____|_____

7. _____|_____   _____|_____

8. _____|_____   _____|_____

9. _____|_____   _____|_____

10. _____|_____   _____|_____

11. _____|_____   _____|_____

12. _____|_____   _____|_____

Analyze: _____

_____

PROBLEM 3.4A or 3.4B

Analyze: _____

_____

PROBLEM 3.5A or 3.5B

ACCOUNT NAME	DEBIT	CREDIT

	DEBIT	CREDIT

PROBLEM 3.5A or 3.5B (continued)

Analyze: _____

CHAPTER 3 CHALLENGE PROBLEM

CHAPTER 3 CHALLENGE PROBLEM (continued)

ACCOUNT NAME	DEBIT	CREDIT

CHAPTER 3 CHALLENGE PROBLEM (continued)

Analyze:

CHAPTER 3 CRITICAL THINKING PROBLEM

CHAPTER 3 CRITICAL THINKING PROBLEM (continued)

CHAPTER 3 CRITICAL THINKING PROBLEM (continued)

_____

_____

_____

_____

_____

_____

_____

_____

_____

_____

_____

_____

_____

_____

_____

_____

_____

Chapter 3 Practice Test Answer Key

Part A True-False	Part B Matching
1. T	1. f
2. F	2. b
3. T	3. d
4. T	4. i
5. T	5. h
6. F	6. c
7. F	7. e
8. F	8. g
9. F	9. a
10. F	
11. T	**Part C Completion**
12. T	1. normal balance
13. T	2. trial balance
14. T	3. slide
15. T	4. transposition
	5. footing

CHAPTER 4 — The General Journal and the General Ledger

STUDY GUIDE

Understanding the Chapter

Objectives

1. Record transactions in the general journal. 2. Prepare compound journal entries. 3. Post journal entries to general ledger accounts. 4. Correct errors made in the journal or ledger. 5. Define the accounting terms new to this chapter.

Reading Assignment

Read Chapter 4 in the textbook. Complete the textbook Section Self Review as you finish reading each section of the chapter, and the Comprehensive Self Review at the end of the chapter. Refer to the Chapter 4 Glossary or to the Glossary at the end of the book to find definitions for terms that are not familiar to you.

Activities

❏ **Thinking Critically** Answer the *Thinking Critically* questions for Caterpillar, Inc., Accounting on the Job, and Managerial Implications.

❏ **Internet Application** Complete the activity for Accounting on the Job.

❏ **Discussion Questions** Answer each assigned discussion question in Chapter 4.

❏ **Exercises** Complete each assigned exercise in Chapter 4. Use the forms provided in this SGWP. The objectives covered by an exercise are given after the exercise number. If you need help with an exercise, review the portion of the chapter related to the objective(s) covered.

❏ **Problems A/B** Complete each assigned problem in Chapter 4. Use the forms provided in this SGWP. The objectives covered by a problem are given after the problem number. If you need help with a problem, review the portion of the chapter related to the objective(s) covered.

❏ **Challenge Problem** Complete the challenge problem as assigned. Use the forms provided in this SGWP.

❏ **Critical Thinking Problem** Complete the critical thinking problem as assigned. Use the forms provided in this SGWP.

❏ **Business Connections** Complete the Business Connections activities as assigned to gain a deeper understanding of Chapter 4 concepts.

Practice Tests

Complete the Practice Tests, which cover the main points in your reading assignment. Compare your answers with those in the Practice Test Answer Key for Chapter 4 at the end of this chapter. If you have answered any questions incorrectly, review the related section of the text.

Part A Matching *For each numbered item, choose the matching term from the box and write the identifying letter in the answer column.*

_____	**1.** A ledger account form that always shows the current balance of an account.	
_____	**2.** A journal entry that consists of more than one debit or more than one credit.	
_____	**3.** A permanent, classified record of all accounts used by a business.	
_____	**4.** Used to analyze transactions but not used to maintain financial records.	
_____	**5.** The process of transferring information from the journal to the ledger.	
_____	**6.** An entry that is made when there is an error in data that has been journalized and posted.	
_____	**7.** Record of original entry.	
_____	**8.** The process of recording transactions in the journal.	
_____	**9.** Invoices and other business forms that contain the original data about transactions.	
_____	**10.** A chain of references that makes it possible to trace information about transactions through an accounting system.	

a. journal

b. source documents

c. posting

d. general ledger

e. T accounts

f. journalizing

g. correcting entry

h. compound entry

i. balance ledger form

j. audit trail

Part B Completion *In the answer column, supply the missing word or words needed to complete each of the following statements.*

_____ **1.** The accountant always records the _____ items first in the Description column of the journal.

_____ **2.** The _____ is always entered at the top of the Date column.

_____ **3.** The accountant enters transactions in the general journal in _____ order.

_____ **4.** The pages in the ledger are usually organized so that the _____ come first.

_____ **5.** If an error is discovered in a journal before the entry is _____, the error can be neatly crossed out and the correct data written above it.

_____ **6.** All the accounts together constitute a(n) _____, or a record of final entry.

_____ **7.** Notations that allow the data in journals and ledgers to be easily traced are called _____.

_____ **8.** Descriptions in the general journal should be complete but _____.

_____ **9.** On the balance ledger form the second money column is used to record _____ amounts.

_____ **10.** On the balance ledger form the first money column is used to record _____ amounts.

Demonstration Problem

On January 1, 2007, Patricia King opened her consulting office and began business as King Consulting Services. Selected transactions for the first month of operations follow.

Instructions

1. Journalize the transactions on page 1 of a general journal. Write the year at the top of the Date column; include an explanation for each entry.

2. Post to the general ledger accounts.

3. Prepare a trial balance.

DATE	TRANSACTIONS
January 1	Patricia King invested $40,000 cash in the business.
2	Issued Check 101 for $3,500 to pay the January rent.
5	Purchased office equipment for $20,500 from Kerry Office Supply, Invoice 4507; issued Check 102 for $5,500 down payment with the balance due in 30 days.
12	Wrote a lease contract for Pamela Davis for $2,000 cash.
15	Performed consulting services for a client, Zant Supply Company, for $15,000 to be received in 30 days.
28	Issued Check 103 for $7,000 for payment to Kerry Office Supply.
29	Issued Check 104 for $3,000 to Patricia King for personal use.
31	Received $9,000 from Zant Supply Company for partial payment of their account.

SOLUTION

	DATE		DESCRIPTION	POST. REF.	DEBIT	CREDIT	
1	**2007**						1
2	**Jan.**	**1**	**Cash**	101	40 0 0 0 00		2
3			**Patricia King, Capital**	301		40 0 0 0 00	3
4			Investment to start business				4
5							5
6		**2**	**Rent Expense**	514	3 5 0 0 00		6
7			**Cash**	101		3 5 0 0 00	7
8			Issued Check 101 for January rent				8
9							9
10		**5**	**Office Equipment**	131	20 5 0 0 00		10
11			**Cash**	101		5 5 0 0 00	11
12			**Accounts Payable**	202		15 0 0 0 00	12
13			Issued Check 102 for office equipment,				13
14			balance due in 30 days.				14
15							15
16		**12**	**Cash**	101	2 0 0 0 00		16
17			**Fees Income**	401		2 0 0 0 00	17
18			Performed services for cash.				18
19							19
20		**15**	**Accounts Receivable**	111	15 0 0 0 00		20
21			**Fees Income**	401		15 0 0 0 00	21
22			Performed services on account.				22
23							23
24		**28**	**Accounts Payable**	202	7 0 0 0 00		24
25			**Cash**	101		7 0 0 0 00	25
26			Paid Invoice 4507, Check 103				26
27							27
28		**29**	**Patricia King, Drawing**	302	3 0 0 0 00		28
29			**Cash**	101		3 0 0 0 00	29
30			Issued Check 104 to owner for personal use.				30
31							31
32		**31**	**Cash**	101	9 0 0 0 00		32
33			**Accounts Receivable**	111		9 0 0 0 00	33
34			Received partial payment				34
35			from Zant Supply Company				35
36							36
37							37
38							38
39							39

44 ■ **Chapter 4**

SOLUTION (continued)

GENERAL LEDGER

ACCOUNT __Cash__   ACCOUNT NO. ____101

DATE		DESCRIPTION	POST. REF.	DEBIT	CREDIT	BALANCE	
						DEBIT	CREDIT
2007							
Jan.	1		J1	40 000 00		40 000 00	
	2		J1		3 500 00	36 500 00	
	5		J1		5 500 00	31 000 00	
	12		J1	2 000 00		33 000 00	
	28		J1		7 000 00	26 000 00	
	29		J1		3 000 00	23 000 00	
	31		J1	9 000 00		32 000 00	

ACCOUNT __Accounts Receivable__   ACCOUNT NO. ____111

DATE		DESCRIPTION	POST. REF.	DEBIT	CREDIT	BALANCE	
						DEBIT	CREDIT
2007							
Jan.	15		J1	15 000 00		15 000 00	
	31		J1		9 000 00	6 000 00	

ACCOUNT __Office Equipment__   ACCOUNT NO. ____131

DATE		DESCRIPTION	POST. REF.	DEBIT	CREDIT	BALANCE	
						DEBIT	CREDIT
2007							
Jan.	5		J1	20 500 00		20 500 00	

ACCOUNT __Accounts Payable__   ACCOUNT NO. ____202

DATE		DESCRIPTION	POST. REF.	DEBIT	CREDIT	BALANCE	
						DEBIT	CREDIT
2007							
Jan.	5		J1		15 000 00		15 000 00
	28		J1	7 000 00			8 000 00

ACCOUNT __Patricia King, Capital__   ACCOUNT NO. ____301

DATE		DESCRIPTION	POST. REF.	DEBIT	CREDIT	BALANCE	
						DEBIT	CREDIT
2007							
Jan.	1		J1		40 000 00		40 000 00

ACCOUNT __Patricia King, Drawing__   ACCOUNT NO. ___302___

DATE		DESCRIPTION	POST. REF.	DEBIT	CREDIT	BALANCE	
						DEBIT	CREDIT
2007							
Jan.	29		J1	3 0 0 0 00		3 0 0 0 00	

ACCOUNT __Fees Income__   ACCOUNT NO. ___401___

DATE		DESCRIPTION	POST. REF.	DEBIT	CREDIT	BALANCE	
						DEBIT	CREDIT
2007							
Jan.	12		J1		2 0 0 0 00		2 0 0 0 00
	15		J1		15 0 0 0 00		17 0 0 0 00

ACCOUNT __Rent Expense__   ACCOUNT NO. ___514___

DATE		DESCRIPTION	POST. REF.	DEBIT	CREDIT	BALANCE	
						DEBIT	CREDIT
2007							
Jan.	2		J1	3 5 0 0 00		3 5 0 0 00	

King Consulting Services
Trial Balance
January 31, 2007

ACCOUNT NAME	DEBIT	CREDIT
Cash	32 0 0 0 00	
Accounts Receivable	6 0 0 0 00	
Office Equipment	20 5 0 0 00	
Accounts Payable		8 0 0 0 00
Patricia King, Capital		40 0 0 0 00
Patricia King, Drawing	3 0 0 0 00	
Fees Income		17 0 0 0 00
Rent Expense	3 5 0 0 00	
Totals	65 0 0 0 00	65 0 0 0 00

WORKING PAPERS

Name _____

EXERCISE 4.1

	Debit	Credit		Debit	Credit		Debit	Credit
1.	_____		5.	_____		8.	_____	
2.	_____		6.	_____		9.	_____	
3.	_____		7.	_____		10.	_____	
4.	_____							

EXERCISE 4.2

GENERAL JOURNAL   PAGE _____

	DATE	DESCRIPTION	POST. REF.	DEBIT	CREDIT	
1	9/1	Cash		62 000		1
2		Capital			62 000	2
3	9/4	Equipment		8 500		3
4		Account Payable			8 500	4
5	9/16	Automobile		22 500		5
6		Cash			22 500	6
7	9/20	Supplies		420		7
8		Cash			420	8
9	9/23	Cash		120		9
10		Supplies			120	10
11	9/30	Account payable		5 600		11
12		Cash			5 600	12
13	9/30	Marilyn James, Drawing		2 000		13
14		Cash			2 000	14
15	9/30	Rent expense		1 200		15
16		Cash			1 200	16
17	9/30	Cash		1 700		17
18		Fees Income			1 700	18
19	9/30	Telephone		207		19
20		Cash			207	20
21						21
22						22
23						23
24						24
25						25
26						26
27						27
28						28
29						29
30						30

EXERCISE 4.2 (continued)

GENERAL JOURNAL

PAGE _____

	DATE		DESCRIPTION	POST. REF.	DEBIT	CREDIT	
1							1
2							2
3							3
4							4
5							5
6							6
7							7
8							8
9							9
10							10
11							11
12							12
13							13
14							14
15							15
16							16
17							17

EXERCISE 4.3

GENERAL LEDGER

ACCOUNT _____   ACCOUNT NO. _____

DATE	DESCRIPTION	POST. REF.	DEBIT	CREDIT	BALANCE	
					DEBIT	CREDIT

Name _____

EXERCISE 4.3 (continued)

GENERAL LEDGER

ACCOUNT _____ ACCOUNT NO. _____

DATE	DESCRIPTION	POST. REF.	DEBIT	CREDIT	BALANCE	
					DEBIT	CREDIT

ACCOUNT _____ ACCOUNT NO. _____

DATE	DESCRIPTION	POST. REF.	DEBIT	CREDIT	BALANCE	
					DEBIT	CREDIT

ACCOUNT _____ ACCOUNT NO. _____

DATE	DESCRIPTION	POST. REF.	DEBIT	CREDIT	BALANCE	
					DEBIT	CREDIT

ACCOUNT _____ ACCOUNT NO. _____

DATE	DESCRIPTION	POST. REF.	DEBIT	CREDIT	BALANCE	
					DEBIT	CREDIT

ACCOUNT _____ ACCOUNT NO. _____

DATE	DESCRIPTION	POST. REF.	DEBIT	CREDIT	BALANCE	
					DEBIT	CREDIT

EXERCISE 4.3 (continued)

GENERAL LEDGER

ACCOUNT _____ ACCOUNT NO. _____

DATE	DESCRIPTION	POST. REF.	DEBIT	CREDIT	BALANCE	
					DEBIT	CREDIT

ACCOUNT _____ ACCOUNT NO. _____

DATE	DESCRIPTION	POST. REF.	DEBIT	CREDIT	BALANCE	
					DEBIT	CREDIT

ACCOUNT _____ ACCOUNT NO. _____

DATE	DESCRIPTION	POST. REF.	DEBIT	CREDIT	BALANCE	
					DEBIT	CREDIT

ACCOUNT _____ ACCOUNT NO. _____

DATE	DESCRIPTION	POST. REF.	DEBIT	CREDIT	BALANCE	
					DEBIT	CREDIT

ACCOUNT _____ ACCOUNT NO. _____

DATE	DESCRIPTION	POST. REF.	DEBIT	CREDIT	BALANCE	
					DEBIT	CREDIT

ACCOUNT _____ ACCOUNT NO. _____

DATE	DESCRIPTION	POST. REF.	DEBIT	CREDIT	BALANCE	
					DEBIT	CREDIT

EXERCISE 4.4

GENERAL JOURNAL

PAGE_____

	DATE	DESCRIPTION	POST. REF.	DEBIT	CREDIT	
1	11/5	Cash		16 000		1
2		Account Receivable		16 000		2
3		Fees Income			32 000	3
4	11/18	Equipment		800		4
5		Supplies		500		5
6		Cash		800		6
7	11/23	Auto Repair Expense		1080	540	7
8		Cash			540	8
9		Auto Repair Expense A/P		1080	540	9
10						10
11						11
12						12
13						13
14						14
15						15
16						16
17						17
18						18
19						19
20						20
21						21
22						22
23						23
24						24
25						25
26						26
27						27
28						28
29						29
30						30
31						31
32						32
33						33
34						34
35						35
36						36
37						37

EXERCISE 4.5

GENERAL JOURNAL   PAGE _____

	DATE		DESCRIPTION	POST. REF.	DEBIT	CREDIT	
1							1
2							2
3							3
4							4
5							5
6							6

EXERCISE 4.6

GENERAL JOURNAL   PAGE _____

	DATE		DESCRIPTION	POST. REF.	DEBIT	CREDIT	
1							1
2							2
3							3
4							4
5							5
6							6

EXTRA FORM

GENERAL JOURNAL   PAGE _____

	DATE		DESCRIPTION	POST. REF.	DEBIT	CREDIT	
1							1
2							2
3							3
4							4
5							5
6							6
7							7
8							8
9							9
10							10
11							11
12							12
13							13

PROBLEM 4.1A or 4.1B

GENERAL JOURNAL
PAGE _____

	DATE	DESCRIPTION	POST. REF.	DEBIT	CREDIT	
1	9/1	Rent Expense		1400		1
2		Cash			1400	2
3	9/5	Cash		2500		3
4		Fees Income			2500	4
5	9/6	~~Cash~~ A/R		2175		5
6		Fees Income			2175	6
7	9/10	Telephone Expense		150		7
8		Cash			150	8
9	9/11	Equipment Repair Expense		210		9
10		Cash			210	10
11	9/12	Account Receivable		800		11
12		~~Cash~~ A/R			800	12
13	9/15	Salaries Expense		4200		13
14		Cash			4200	14
15	9/18	Supplies		500		15
16		~~Equipmt~~ Cash			500	16
17	9/19	~~Account Payable~~		2250		17
18		~~Cash~~ A/P			2250	18
19	9/20	Equipment		690		19
20		Cash			690	20
21	9/21	Account Receivable		850		21
22		Cash			850	22
23	9/21	Equipment Repair Expense		212		23
24		Cash			212	24
25	9/22	Cash		3260		25
26		Fees Income			3260	26
27	9/23	~~Cash~~ A/R		4810		27
28		Fees Income			4810	28
29	9/26	Supplies		460		29
30		Cash			460	30
31	9/28	Utilities Expense		575		31
32		Cash			575	32
33	9/30	Salaries Expense		4200		33
34		Cash			4200	34
35	9/30	R. H. Drawing		1000		35
36		Cash			1000	36
37						37
38						38

PROBLEM 4.1A or 4.1B (continued)

GENERAL JOURNAL   PAGE _____

	DATE		DESCRIPTION	POST. REF.	DEBIT	CREDIT	
1							1
2							2
3							3
4							4
5							5
6							6
7							7
8							8
9							9
10							10
11							11
12							12
13							13
14							14
15							15
16							16
17							17
18							18
19							19
20							20
21							21
22							22
23							23
24							24
25							25
26							26
27							27
28							28
29							29
30							30
31							31
32							32
33							33
34							34
35							35
36							36
37							37

Analyze: _____

PROBLEM 4.2A or 4.2B

Name _____

GENERAL JOURNAL

PAGE _____

	DATE	DESCRIPTION	POST. REF.	DEBIT	CREDIT	
1	10/1	Cash		70 000		1
2		Capital			70 000	2
3	10/2	Rent Expense		2 250		3
4		Cash			2 250	4
5	10/5	Office Equipment		14 000		5
6		Account Receivable			14 000	6
7	10/6	Art Equipment		4 350		7
8		Cash			4 350	8
9	10/7	Supplies		1 070		9
10		Cash			1 070	10
11	10/10	Office Cleaning Expense		425		11
12		Cash			425	12
13	10/12					13
14						14
15						15
16	10/15	Accounts Payable		300		16
17		Cash			300	17
18	10/18	Office Equipment		2 050		18
19		Cash			1 025	19
20		A/P			1 025	20
21	10/20	Office Equipment		7 000		21
22		Cash			7 000	22
23	10/26	Account Receivable		3 875		23
24		Fee Income			3 875	24
25	10/27	Telephone Expense		250		25
26		Cash			250	26
27	10/30	Account Receivable		3 200		27
28		Cash			3 200	28
29	10/30	Utilities Expense		592		29
30		Cash			592	30
31	10/30	Salaries Expense		7 550		31
32		Cash			7 550	32
33						33
34						34
35						35
36						36
37						37

PROBLEM 4.2A or 4.2B (continued)

GENERAL JOURNAL   PAGE _____

	DATE		DESCRIPTION	POST. REF.	DEBIT	CREDIT	
1							1
2							2
3							3
4							4
5							5
6							6
7							7
8							8
9							9
10							10
11							11
12							12
13							13
14							14
15							15
16							16
17							17
18							18
19							19
20							20
21							21
22							22
23							23
24							24
25							25
26							26
27							27
28							28
29							29
30							30
31							31
32							32
33							33
34							34
35							35
36							36
37							37

PROBLEM 4.2A or 4.2B (continued)

GENERAL LEDGER

ACCOUNT _____ ACCOUNT NO. _____

DATE	DESCRIPTION	POST. REF.	DEBIT	CREDIT	BALANCE	
					DEBIT	CREDIT

ACCOUNT _____ ACCOUNT NO. _____

DATE	DESCRIPTION	POST. REF.	DEBIT	CREDIT	BALANCE	
					DEBIT	CREDIT

ACCOUNT _____ ACCOUNT NO. _____

DATE	DESCRIPTION	POST. REF.	DEBIT	CREDIT	BALANCE	
					DEBIT	CREDIT

ACCOUNT _____ ACCOUNT NO. _____

DATE	DESCRIPTION	POST. REF.	DEBIT	CREDIT	BALANCE	
					DEBIT	CREDIT

PROBLEM 4.2A or 4.2B (continued)

GENERAL LEDGER

ACCOUNT _____ ACCOUNT NO. _____

DATE	DESCRIPTION	POST. REF.	DEBIT	CREDIT	BALANCE	
					DEBIT	CREDIT

ACCOUNT _____ ACCOUNT NO. _____

DATE	DESCRIPTION	POST. REF.	DEBIT	CREDIT	BALANCE	
					DEBIT	CREDIT

ACCOUNT _____ ACCOUNT NO. _____

DATE	DESCRIPTION	POST. REF.	DEBIT	CREDIT	BALANCE	
					DEBIT	CREDIT

ACCOUNT _____ ACCOUNT NO. _____

DATE	DESCRIPTION	POST. REF.	DEBIT	CREDIT	BALANCE	
					DEBIT	CREDIT

ACCOUNT _____ ACCOUNT NO. _____

DATE	DESCRIPTION	POST. REF.	DEBIT	CREDIT	BALANCE	
					DEBIT	CREDIT

PROBLEM 4.2A or 4.2B (continued)

GENERAL LEDGER

ACCOUNT _____ ACCOUNT NO. _____

DATE	DESCRIPTION	POST. REF.	DEBIT	CREDIT	BALANCE DEBIT	BALANCE CREDIT

ACCOUNT _____ ACCOUNT NO. _____

DATE	DESCRIPTION	POST. REF.	DEBIT	CREDIT	BALANCE DEBIT	BALANCE CREDIT

ACCOUNT _____ ACCOUNT NO. _____

DATE	DESCRIPTION	POST. REF.	DEBIT	CREDIT	BALANCE DEBIT	BALANCE CREDIT

ACCOUNT _____ ACCOUNT NO. _____

DATE	DESCRIPTION	POST. REF.	DEBIT	CREDIT	BALANCE DEBIT	BALANCE CREDIT

ACCOUNT _____ ACCOUNT NO. _____

DATE	DESCRIPTION	POST. REF.	DEBIT	CREDIT	BALANCE DEBIT	BALANCE CREDIT

Analyze: _____

PROBLEM 4.3A or 4.3B

_____
_____
_____
_____
_____
_____

Analyze: _____
_____

PROBLEM 4.4A or 4.4B

GENERAL JOURNAL   PAGE _____

	DATE	DESCRIPTION	POST. REF.	DEBIT	CREDIT	
1	11/1					1
2						2
3						3
4						4
5						5
6						6
7						7
8						8
9						9
10						10
11						11
12						12
13						13
14						14
15						15
16						16
17						17
18						18
19						19
20						20
21						21
22						22
23						23
24						24
25						25
26						26

Name _____

PROBLEM 4.4A or 4.4B (continued)

GENERAL LEDGER

ACCOUNT _____ ACCOUNT NO. _____

DATE	DESCRIPTION	POST. REF.	DEBIT	CREDIT	BALANCE	
					DEBIT	CREDIT

ACCOUNT _____ ACCOUNT NO. _____

DATE	DESCRIPTION	POST. REF.	DEBIT	CREDIT	BALANCE	
					DEBIT	CREDIT

ACCOUNT _____ ACCOUNT NO. _____

DATE	DESCRIPTION	POST. REF.	DEBIT	CREDIT	BALANCE	
					DEBIT	CREDIT

ACCOUNT _____ ACCOUNT NO. _____

DATE	DESCRIPTION	POST. REF.	DEBIT	CREDIT	BALANCE	
					DEBIT	CREDIT

ACCOUNT _____ ACCOUNT NO. _____

DATE	DESCRIPTION	POST. REF.	DEBIT	CREDIT	BALANCE	
					DEBIT	CREDIT

PROBLEM 4.4A or 4.4B (continued)

GENERAL LEDGER

ACCOUNT _____ ACCOUNT NO. _____

	DATE	DESCRIPTION	POST. REF.	DEBIT	CREDIT	BALANCE	
						DEBIT	CREDIT

ACCOUNT _____ ACCOUNT NO. _____

	DATE	DESCRIPTION	POST. REF.	DEBIT	CREDIT	BALANCE	
						DEBIT	CREDIT

ACCOUNT _____ ACCOUNT NO. _____

	DATE	DESCRIPTION	POST. REF.	DEBIT	CREDIT	BALANCE	
						DEBIT	CREDIT

ACCOUNT _____ ACCOUNT NO. _____

	DATE	DESCRIPTION	POST. REF.	DEBIT	CREDIT	BALANCE	
						DEBIT	CREDIT

Analyze: _____

_____

EXTRA FORM

GENERAL LEDGER

ACCOUNT _____ ACCOUNT NO. _____

	DATE	DESCRIPTION	POST. REF.	DEBIT	CREDIT	BALANCE	
						DEBIT	CREDIT

CHAPTER 4 CHALLENGE PROBLEM

GENERAL JOURNAL

PAGE _____

	DATE	DESCRIPTION	POST. REF.	DEBIT	CREDIT	
1	6/1	Cash		30 000		1
2		Capital			30 000	2
3	6/2	Rent Expense		1 800		3
4		Cash			1 800	4
5	6/3	Office furniture		12 000		5
6		Cash			4 000	6
7		A/P			8 000	7
8	6/4	Supplies		1 600		8
9		Cash			1 600	9
10	6/6	Cash		6 000		10
11		Fee Income			6 000	11
12	6/7	Advertising Expense		2 000		12
13		Cash			2 000	13
14	6/8	Recording equipment		15 000		14
15		Cash			5 000	15
16		A/P			10 000	16
17	6/10	A/R		4 900		17
18		Fee Income			4 900	18
19	6/11	A/P		3 000		19
20		Cash			3 000	20
21	6/12	Cash		9 000		21
22		Fee Income			9 000	22
23	6/15	Salaries Expense		5 000		23
24		Cash			5 000	24
25	6/18	Cash		4 000		25
26		A/R			4 000	26
27	6/20	A/P		6 000		27
28		Cash			6 000	28
29	6/23	Telephone ~~Utilities~~ Expense		350		29
30		Cash			350	30
31	6/27	Utilities Expense		800		31
32		Cash			800	32
33	6/28	Drawing		4 000		33
34		Cash			4 000	34
35	6/30	Salaries Expense		5 000		35
36		Cash			5 000	36
37						37

CHAPTER 4 CHALLENGE PROBLEM (continued)

GENERAL JOURNAL   PAGE _____

	DATE		DESCRIPTION	POST. REF.	DEBIT	CREDIT	
1							1
2							2
3							3
4							4
5							5
6							6
7							7
8							8
9							9
10							10
11							11
12							12
13							13
14							14
15							15
16							16
17							17
18							18
19							19
20							20
21							21
22							22
23							23
24							24
25							25
26							26
27							27
28							28
29							29
30							30
31							31
32							32
33							33
34							34
35							35
36							36
37							37

CHAPTER 4 CHALLENGE PROBLEM (continued)

GENERAL JOURNAL

PAGE _____

	DATE	DESCRIPTION	POST. REF.	DEBIT	CREDIT	
1						1
2						2
3						3
4						4
5						5
6						6
7						7
8						8
9						9
10						10
11						11
12						12
13						13
14						14

GENERAL LEDGER

ACCOUNT _____ ACCOUNT NO. _____

DATE	DESCRIPTION	POST. REF.	DEBIT	CREDIT	BALANCE DEBIT	BALANCE CREDIT
6/1						

CHAPTER 4 CHALLENGE PROBLEM (continued)

GENERAL LEDGER

ACCOUNT _____ ACCOUNT NO. _____

DATE	DESCRIPTION	POST. REF.	DEBIT	CREDIT	BALANCE	
					DEBIT	CREDIT

ACCOUNT _____ ACCOUNT NO. _____

DATE	DESCRIPTION	POST. REF.	DEBIT	CREDIT	BALANCE	
					DEBIT	CREDIT

ACCOUNT _____ ACCOUNT NO. _____

DATE	DESCRIPTION	POST. REF.	DEBIT	CREDIT	BALANCE	
					DEBIT	CREDIT

ACCOUNT _____ ACCOUNT NO. _____

DATE	DESCRIPTION	POST. REF.	DEBIT	CREDIT	BALANCE	
					DEBIT	CREDIT

ACCOUNT _____ ACCOUNT NO. _____

DATE	DESCRIPTION	POST. REF.	DEBIT	CREDIT	BALANCE	
					DEBIT	CREDIT

CHAPTER 4 CHALLENGE PROBLEM (continued)

GENERAL LEDGER

ACCOUNT _____ ACCOUNT NO. _____

	DATE	DESCRIPTION	POST. REF.	DEBIT	CREDIT	BALANCE	
						DEBIT	CREDIT

ACCOUNT _____ ACCOUNT NO. _____

	DATE	DESCRIPTION	POST. REF.	DEBIT	CREDIT	BALANCE	
						DEBIT	CREDIT

ACCOUNT _____ ACCOUNT NO. _____

	DATE	DESCRIPTION	POST. REF.	DEBIT	CREDIT	BALANCE	
						DEBIT	CREDIT

ACCOUNT _____ ACCOUNT NO. _____

	DATE	DESCRIPTION	POST. REF.	DEBIT	CREDIT	BALANCE	
						DEBIT	CREDIT

ACCOUNT _____ ACCOUNT NO. _____

	DATE	DESCRIPTION	POST. REF.	DEBIT	CREDIT	BALANCE	
						DEBIT	CREDIT

Name _____

CHAPTER 4 CHALLENGE PROBLEM (continued)

GENERAL LEDGER

ACCOUNT _____ ACCOUNT NO. _____

DATE	DESCRIPTION	POST. REF.	DEBIT	CREDIT	BALANCE DEBIT	BALANCE CREDIT

ACCOUNT _____ ACCOUNT NO. _____

DATE	DESCRIPTION	POST. REF.	DEBIT	CREDIT	BALANCE DEBIT	BALANCE CREDIT

ACCOUNT _____ ACCOUNT NO. _____

DATE	DESCRIPTION	POST. REF.	DEBIT	CREDIT	BALANCE DEBIT	BALANCE CREDIT

EXTRA FORMS

GENERAL LEDGER

ACCOUNT _____ ACCOUNT NO. _____

DATE	DESCRIPTION	POST. REF.	DEBIT	CREDIT	BALANCE DEBIT	BALANCE CREDIT

ACCOUNT _____ ACCOUNT NO. _____

DATE	DESCRIPTION	POST. REF.	DEBIT	CREDIT	BALANCE DEBIT	BALANCE CREDIT

CHAPTER 4 CHALLENGE PROBLEM (continued)

ACCOUNT NAME	DEBIT	CREDIT
Revenues		
Fees Income		2580000
Total Revenues		2580000
Expense		
Depreciation expense	55000	
Insurance expense	250000	
Salaries expense	780000	
Supplies expense	800000	
Utilities expense	80000	
Total expense		1965000
Net Income		615000

Statement of ower's Equity

Capital 1/1/97		6300000
Add net income 1/97		615000
Less withdrawals 1/97		360000
		15 S 50
Capital 1/31/97		

CHAPTER 4 CHALLENGE PROBLEM (continued)

Balance Sheet

Assets						
Cash	26000	00				
A/R	5 2000	00				
Supplies	1 600	00				
Prepaid Insurance	1250	00				
Equipment	27000	00				
Less. Accum Depr				550	00	
Total Assets	71750	00				
Liab and equity						
A/P				6 2000	00	
Capital				65550	00	
Total Liab & Equity				71750	00	

CHAPTER 4 CRITICAL THINKING PROBLEM

CHAPTER 4 CRITICAL THINKING PROBLEM (continued)

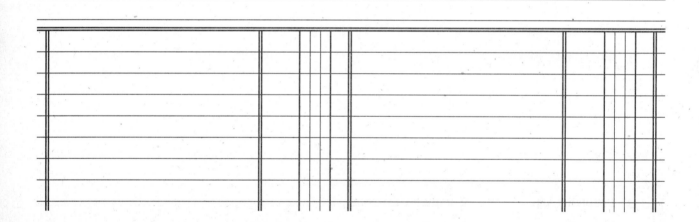

Chapter 4 Practice Test Answer Key

Part A Matching	Part B Completion
1. i	1. debit
2. h	2. year
3. d	3. chronological or date
4. e	4. assets or balance sheet accounts
5. c	5. posted
6. g	6. ledger
7. a	7. posting references
8. f	8. brief or concise
9. b	9. credit
10. j	10. debit

Adjustments and the Worksheet

STUDY GUIDE

Understanding the Chapter

Objectives
1. Complete a trial balance on a worksheet. **2.** Prepare adjustments for unrecorded business transactions. **3.** Complete the worksheet. **4.** Prepare an income statement, statement of owner's equity, and balance sheet from the completed worksheet. **5.** Journalize and post the adjusting entries. **6.** Define the accounting terms new to this chapter.

Reading Assignment
Read Chapter 5 in the textbook. Complete the textbook Section Self Review as you finish reading each section of the chapter, and the Comprehensive Self Review at the end of the chapter. Refer to the Chapter 5 Glossary or to the Glossary at the end of the book to find definitions for terms that are not familiar to you.

Activities

❑ **Thinking Critically**
Answer the *Thinking Critically* questions for Boeing, Computers in Accounting, and Managerial Implications.

❑ **Internet Application**
Complete the activity for Computers in Accounting.

❑ **Discussion Questions**
Answer each assigned discussion question in Chapter 5.

❑ **Exercises**
Complete each assigned exercise in Chapter 5. Use the forms provided in this SGWP. The objectives covered by an exercise are given after the exercise number. If you need help with an exercise, review the portion of the chapter related to the objective(s) covered.

❑ **Problems A/B**
Complete each assigned problem in Chapter 5. Use the forms provided in this SGWP. The objectives covered by a problem are given after the problem number. If you need help with a problem, review the portion of the chapter related to the objective(s) covered.

❑ **Challenge Problem**
Complete the challenge problem as assigned. Use the forms provided in this SGWP.

❑ **Critical Thinking Problem**
Complete the critical thinking problem as assigned. Use the forms provided in this SGWP.

❑ **Business Connections**
Complete the Business Connections activities as assigned to gain a deeper understanding of Chapter 5 concepts.

Practice Tests
Complete the Practice Tests, which cover the main points in your reading assignment. Compare your answers with those in the Practice Test Answer Key for Chapter 5 at the end of this chapter. If you have answered any questions incorrectly, review the related section of the text.

Part A True-False *For each of the following statements, circle T in the answer column if the statement is true or F if the statement is false.*

T   F   **1.** The balances of the expense accounts are normally transferred to the Income Statement Debit column of the worksheet.

T   F   **2.** When the Balance Sheet columns of the worksheet are first added, the total of the Debit column should equal the total of the Credit column.

T   F   **3.** After the net income (or net loss) is computed in the Income Statement section of the worksheet, this amount is transferred to the Balance Sheet section of the worksheet.

T   F   **4.** On a worksheet, the difference between the Debit and Credit Column totals in the Income Statement section must equal the difference between the Debit and Credit column totals in the Balance Sheet section.

T   F   **5.** The Income Statement columns and Balance Sheet columns provide the figures for preparing the financial statements.

T   F   **6.** The ledger must be in balance before financial statements are prepared.

T   F   **7.** Accountants use a worksheet as a means of organizing their figures quickly.

T   F   **8.** The first two money columns of the worksheet contain a trial balance of the general ledger accounts.

T   F   **9.** Asset account balances from the trial balance are normally transferred to the Income Statement Debit column of the worksheet.

T   F   **10.** Liability account balances from the trial balance are normally transferred to the Balance Sheet credit column of the worksheet.

Part B Matching   *For each numbered item, choose the matching term from the box and write the identifying letter in the answer column.*

_____   **1.** A form used to organize the amounts needed to prepare the financial statements

_____   **2.** The term used when referring to an account in which there is an excess of credits over debits

_____   **3.** The term used when the total of the debit amounts in the general ledger and the total of the credit amounts are equal

_____   **4.** The term used for an account with an excess of debits over credits

_____   **5.** A way to test the accuracy of the figures recorded in the general ledger

_____   **6.** Assets = Liabilities + Owner's Equity

a. Worksheet
b. Trial balance
c. Debit balance
d. Fundamental accounting equation
e. Credit balance
f. In balance

Demonstration Problem

The general ledger accounts listed on the worksheet for the Environmental Design Company on January 31, 2007, show the results of the first month of operation.

Instructions

1. Record the following adjustments in the Adjustments section of the worksheet using the information below.

   a. Supplies used during the month, $1,475.

   b. The amount in the **Prepaid Rent** account represents a payment made on January 1 for the rent for 12 months.

   c. The equipment, purchased in January, has an estimated useful life of 10 years with no salvage value. The firm uses the straight-line method of depreciation.

2. Complete the worksheet.

3. Journalize and post the adjusting entries. Use journal page number 2.

Environmental Design Company

Worksheet

Month Ended January 31, 2007

ACCOUNT NAME	TRIAL BALANCE		ADJUSTMENTS		ADJUSTED TRIAL BALANCE		INCOME STATEMENT		BALANCE SHEET	
	DEBIT	CREDIT	DEBIT	CREDIT	DEBIT	CREDIT	DEBIT	CREDIT	DEBIT	CREDIT
Cash	12,450.00				12,450.00				12,450.00	
Accounts Receivable	16,900.00				16,900.00				16,900.00	
Supplies	2,900.00			(a)1,475.00	1,425.00				1,425.00	
Prepaid Rent	42,000.00			(b)3,500.00	38,500.00				38,500.00	
Equipment	42,000.00				42,000.00				42,000.00	
Accum. Depr.—Equipment				(c) 350.00		350.00				350.00
Accounts Payable		26,800.00				26,800.00				26,800.00
John Peoples, Capital		49,200.00				49,200.00				49,200.00
John Peoples, Drawing	3,000.00				3,000.00				3,000.00	
Fees Income		75,505.00				75,505.00		75,505.00		
Advertising Expense	3,800.00				3,800.00		3,800.00			
Insurance Expense	4,000.00				4,000.00		4,000.00			
Salaries Expense	22,500.00				22,500.00		22,500.00			
Supplies Expense			(a)1,475.00		1,475.00		1,475.00			
Rent Expense			(b)3,500.00		3,500.00		3,500.00			
Telephone Expense	875.00				875.00		875.00			
Utilities Expense	1,080.00				1,080.00		1,080.00			
Depr. Expense—Equipment			(c) 350.00		350.00		350.00			
Totals	151,505.00	151,505.00	5,325.00	5,325.00	151,855.00	151,855.00	37,580.00	75,505.00	114,275.00	76,350.00
Net Income							37,925.00			37,925.00
							75,505.00	75,505.00	114,275.00	114,275.00

SOLUTION (continued)

GENERAL JOURNAL   PAGE ___2___

	DATE		DESCRIPTION	POST. REF.	DEBIT	CREDIT	
1			**Adjusting Entries**				1
2	2007						2
3	Jan.	31	Supplies Expense	518	1 4 7 5 00		3
4			Supplies	121		1 4 7 5 00	4
5							5
6		31	**Rent Expense**	519	3 5 0 0 00		6
7			Prepaid Rent	131		3 5 0 0 00	7
8							8
9		31	**Depreciation Expense—Equipment**	524	3 5 0 00		9
10			**Accumulated Depreciation—Equipment**	142		3 5 0 00	10
11							11

GENERAL LEDGER (PARTIAL)

ACCOUNT __Supplies__   ACCOUNT NO. ___121___

DATE		DESCRIPTION	POST. REF.	DEBIT	CREDIT	BALANCE DEBIT	BALANCE CREDIT
2007							
Jan.	3		J1	2 9 0 0 00		2 9 0 0 00	
	31	Adjusting	J2		1 4 7 5 00	1 4 2 5 00	

ACCOUNT __Prepaid Rent__   ACCOUNT NO. ___131___

DATE		DESCRIPTION	POST. REF.	DEBIT	CREDIT	BALANCE DEBIT	BALANCE CREDIT
2007							
Jan.	2		J1	42 0 0 0 00		42 0 0 0 00	
	31	Adjusting	J2		3 5 0 0 00	38 5 0 0 00	

ACCOUNT __Accumulated Depreciation—Equipment__   ACCOUNT NO. ___142___

DATE		DESCRIPTION	POST. REF.	DEBIT	CREDIT	BALANCE DEBIT	BALANCE CREDIT
2007							
Jan.	31	Adjusting	J2		3 5 0 00		3 5 0 00

SOLUTION (continued)

GENERAL LEDGER (PARTIAL)

ACCOUNT **Supplies Expense** ACCOUNT NO. **518**

DATE		DESCRIPTION	POST. REF.	DEBIT	CREDIT	BALANCE DEBIT	BALANCE CREDIT
2007							
Jan.	31	Adjusting	J2	1 4 7 5 00		1 4 7 5 00	

ACCOUNT **Rent Expense** ACCOUNT NO. **519**

DATE		DESCRIPTION	POST. REF.	DEBIT	CREDIT	BALANCE DEBIT	BALANCE CREDIT
2007							
Jan.	31	Adjusting	J2	3 5 0 0 00		3 5 0 0 00	

ACCOUNT **Depreciation Expense—Equipment** ACCOUNT NO. **524**

DATE		DESCRIPTION	POST. REF.	DEBIT	CREDIT	BALANCE DEBIT	BALANCE CREDIT
2007							
Jan.	31	Adjusting	J2	3 5 0 00		3 5 0 00	

WORKING PAPERS

Name _____

EXERCISE 5.1

1. June 3L, 2007 Debit Rent Exp 1500
   and credit prepaid Rent 1500

2. Debit Supplies^exp 1475 (2375-900=1475)
   credit Supplies 1475

3. Debit Depr Exp
   Cr accum Depr

   $$\frac{27,000 \; \emptyset\emptyset}{120} \rightarrow \boxed{225}$$

EXERCISE 5.2

1. Debit ~~___ debit insurance expen~~ ~~___~~ = $250
   Credit prepaid insurance $___ ~~___~~ = $25

   ~~___~~ = $250

2. ~~December 31, 2007 debit advertising expense $54~~
   ~~Credit advertising ___ ___~~

   ^prepaid $2 = $450

EXERCISE 5.3

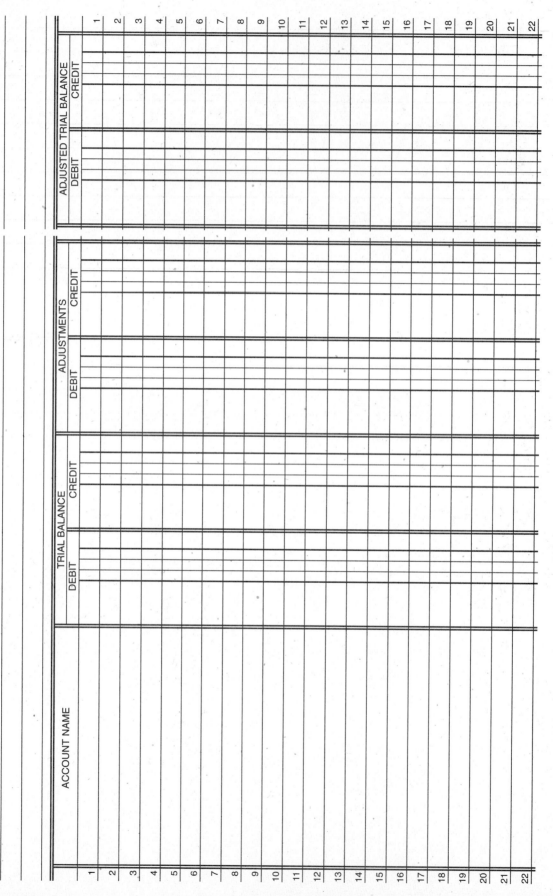

EXERCISE 5.4

_____

_____

_____

_____

_____

_____

_____

_____

_____

_____

_____

_____

_____

_____

EXERCISE 5.5

GENERAL JOURNAL

PAGE _____

	DATE	DESCRIPTION	POST. REF.	DEBIT	CREDIT	
1	12/31	Supplies Exp.		2500		1
2		Supplies			2500	2
3	12/31	Ins. Exp		1800		3
4		Prepaid Ins.			1800	4
5	12/31	Depreciation Exp		1200		5
6		Accum Depr.			1200	6
7						7
8						8
9						9
10						10
11						11

GENERAL LEDGER

ACCOUNT __Supplies__   ACCOUNT NO. ___121__

DATE	DESCRIPTION	POST. REF.	DEBIT	CREDIT	BALANCE DEBIT	BALANCE CREDIT

ACCOUNT __Prepaid Insurance__   ACCOUNT NO. ___131__

DATE	DESCRIPTION	POST. REF.	DEBIT	CREDIT	BALANCE DEBIT	BALANCE CREDIT

ACCOUNT __Accumulated Depreciation—Equipment__   ACCOUNT NO. ___142__

DATE	DESCRIPTION	POST. REF.	DEBIT	CREDIT	BALANCE DEBIT	BALANCE CREDIT

EXERCISE 5.5 (continued)

GENERAL LEDGER

ACCOUNT __Depreciation Expense—Equipment_____ ACCOUNT NO. __517__

DATE	DESCRIPTION	POST. REF.	DEBIT	CREDIT	BALANCE DEBIT	CREDIT

ACCOUNT __Insurance Expense_____ ACCOUNT NO. __521__

DATE	DESCRIPTION	POST. REF.	DEBIT	CREDIT	BALANCE DEBIT	CREDIT

ACCOUNT __Supplies Expense_____ ACCOUNT NO. __523__

DATE	DESCRIPTION	POST. REF.	DEBIT	CREDIT	BALANCE DEBIT	CREDIT

EXTRA FORMS

ACCOUNT _____ ACCOUNT NO. _____

DATE	DESCRIPTION	POST. REF.	DEBIT	CREDIT	BALANCE DEBIT	CREDIT

ACCOUNT _____ ACCOUNT NO. _____

DATE	DESCRIPTION	POST. REF.	DEBIT	CREDIT	BALANCE DEBIT	CREDIT

Expense is always debit.

PROBLEM 5.1A or 5.1B

	ACCOUNT NAME	TRIAL BALANCE DEBIT	TRIAL BALANCE CREDIT	ADJUSTMENTS DEBIT	ADJUSTMENTS CREDIT
1	Cash	26 000 00			
2	Accounts Receivable	5 200 00			
3	Supplies	9 600 00			8 000 00
4	Prepaid Insurance	15 000 00		2 500 00	2 500 00
5	Equipment	27 000 00			
6	Accumulated-Depr-Equipm.				550 00
7	Accounts payable		6 200 00		
8	Julie Denton-Capital		63 500 00		
9	Julie Denton-Drawing	3 600 00			
10	Fees Income		25 800 00		
11	Depreciation exp- Equipm			550 00	
12	Insurance Expense			2 500 00	
13	Salaries Expense	7 800 00		2 550 00	
14	Supplies Expense			8 000 00	
15	Utilities Expense	8 500 00			
16	Totals	95 000 00	95 000 00	11 050 00	11 050 00
17					
18	Net Income				
19					
20					
21					
22					
23					
24					
25					
26					
27					
28					
29					
30					
31					
32					

PROBLEM 5.1A or 5.1B (continued)

| ADJUSTED TRIAL BALANCE | | INCOME STATEMENT | | BALANCE SHEET | | |
DEBIT	CREDIT	DEBIT	CREDIT	DEBIT	CREDIT	
26,000 00				26,000 00		1
5,200 00				5,200 00		2
1,600 00				1,600 00		3
12,500 00				12,500 00		4
27,000 00				27,000 00		5
	550 00				550 00	6
	6,200 00				6,200 00	7
	63,000 00				63,000 00	8
3,600 00				3,600 00		9
	25,800 00		25,800 00			10
550 00		550 00				11
2,500 00		2,500 00				12
7,800 00		7,800 00				13
8,000 00		8,000 00				14
800 00		800 00				15
95,550 00	95,550 00	19,650 00	25,800 00	75,900 00	69,750 00	16
						17
		6,150 00			6,150 00	18
		25,800 00		75,900 00	75,900 00	19
						20
						21
						22
						23
						24
						25
						26
						27
						28
						29
						30
						31
						32

Analyze: _____

PROBLEM 5.2A or 5.2B

_____

	ACCOUNT NAME	TRIAL BALANCE		ADJUSTMENTS	
		DEBIT	CREDIT	DEBIT	CREDIT
1					
2					
3					
4					
5					
6					
7					
8					
9					
10					
11					
12					
13					
14					
15					
16					
17					
18					
19					
20					
21					
22					
23					
24					
25					
26					
27					
28					
29					
30					
31					
32					

Name _____

PROBLEM 5.2A or 5.2B (continued)

_____
_____

ADJUSTED TRIAL BALANCE		INCOME STATEMENT		BALANCE SHEET		
DEBIT	CREDIT	DEBIT	CREDIT	DEBIT	CREDIT	
						1
						2
						3
						4
						5
						6
						7
						8
						9
						10
						11
						12
						13
						14
						15
						16
						17
						18
						19
						20
						21
						22
						23
						24
						25
						26
						27
						28
						29
						30
						31
						32

Analyze: _____
_____

Account	Db	Cr
Revenues		
Fees Income		39 750 00
Total Revenues		39 750 00
Statement of owner's Equity		
Capital 12/31/07		54 000 00
Add Net income 12/07		25 650 00
Less withdrawal 12/07		3 600 00
Capital 12/31/07		76 050 00

Balance Sheet	Db	Cr
Assets		
Cash	38 600 00	
A/R	6 000 00	
Supplies	2 050 00	
Prepaid Advertising	6 000 00	
Equipment	30 000 00	
Less Accum Depr		600 00
Total Assets	82 050 00	

PROBLEM 5.3A or 5.3B (continued)

Analyze: _____

PROBLEM 5.4A or 5.4B

	ACCOUNT NAME	TRIAL BALANCE		ADJUSTMENTS	
		DEBIT	CREDIT	DEBIT	CREDIT
1	Cash	17 750 00			
2	A/R	6 800 00			
3	Supplies	3 875 00			3 325 00
4	Prepaid advertising	4 200 00			1 050 00
5	Prepaid Rent	9 600 00			800 00
6	Equipment	10 800 00			
7	Accum. Depr.-Equipm				90 00
8	A/P		7 775 00		
9	Capital		30 000 00		
10	drawing				
11	Fees income		33 800 00		
12	Advertising Exp.			1 050 00	
13	Depr. Exp.-Equip			90 00	
14	Rent Exp.			800 00	
15	Salaries exp.	4 850 00			
16	Supplies exp			3 325 00	
17	Utilities exp	700 00			
18	Totals	61 575 00	61 575 00	5 265 00	5 265 00
19					
20					
21					
22					
23					
24					
25					
26					
27					
28					
29					
30					
31					
32					

PROBLEM 5.4A or 5.4B (continued)

_____
_____

	ADJUSTED TRIAL BALANCE		INCOME STATEMENT		BALANCE SHEET		
	DEBIT	CREDIT	DEBIT	CREDIT	DEBIT	CREDIT	
1	17 750 00				17 750 00		
2	6 300 00				6 300 00		
3	550 00				550 00		
4	3 150 00				3 150 00		
5	8 800 00				8 800 00		
6	10 800 00				10 800 00		
7		90 00				90 00	
8		7 775 00				7 775 00	
9		30 000 00				30 000 00	
10	3 500 00				3 500 00		
11		23 800 00		23 800 00			
12	1 050 00		1 050 00				
13	90 00		90 00				
14	800 00		800 00				
15	4 850 00		4 850 00				
16	3 325 00		3 325 00				
17	700 00		700 00				
18	61 665 00	61 665 00	10 815 00	23 800 00	50 850 00	37 865 00	
19			12 985 00			12 985 00	
20			23 800 00			50 850 00	

PROBLEM 5.4A or 5.4B (continued)

Revenues			
Fee Income			23800 00
Total Revenues			23800 00

PROBLEM 5.4A or 5.4B (continued)

PROBLEM 5.4A or 5.4B (continued)

GENERAL JOURNAL   PAGE _____

	DATE	DESCRIPTION	POST. REF.	DEBIT	CREDIT	
1						1
2						2
3						3
4						4
5						5
6						6
7						7
8						8
9						9
10						10
11						11
12						12
13						13
14						14

GENERAL LEDGER

ACCOUNT _____ ACCOUNT NO. _____

DATE	DESCRIPTION	POST. REF.	DEBIT	CREDIT	BALANCE DEBIT	BALANCE CREDIT

ACCOUNT _____ ACCOUNT NO. _____

DATE	DESCRIPTION	POST. REF.	DEBIT	CREDIT	BALANCE DEBIT	BALANCE CREDIT

ACCOUNT _____ ACCOUNT NO. _____

DATE	DESCRIPTION	POST. REF.	DEBIT	CREDIT	BALANCE DEBIT	BALANCE CREDIT

PROBLEM 5.4A or 5.4B (continued)

GENERAL LEDGER

ACCOUNT _____ ACCOUNT NO. _____

DATE		DESCRIPTION	POST. REF.	DEBIT	CREDIT	BALANCE	
						DEBIT	CREDIT

ACCOUNT _____ ACCOUNT NO. _____

DATE		DESCRIPTION	POST. REF.	DEBIT	CREDIT	BALANCE	
						DEBIT	CREDIT

ACCOUNT _____ ACCOUNT NO. _____

DATE		DESCRIPTION	POST. REF.	DEBIT	CREDIT	BALANCE	
						DEBIT	CREDIT

ACCOUNT _____ ACCOUNT NO. _____

DATE		DESCRIPTION	POST. REF.	DEBIT	CREDIT	BALANCE	
						DEBIT	CREDIT

ACCOUNT _____ ACCOUNT NO. _____

DATE		DESCRIPTION	POST. REF.	DEBIT	CREDIT	BALANCE	
						DEBIT	CREDIT

Analyze: _____

_____

INC st. Subtract. Cr BDb together

CHAPTER 5 CHALLENGE PROBLEM

	ACCOUNT NAME	TRIAL BALANCE		ADJUSTMENTS	
		DEBIT	CREDIT	DEBIT	CREDIT
1	Cash	18 475			
2	A/R	3 400			
3	Supplies	2 150			1050
4	Prep. Ins	15000			2500
5	Equipmt.	24000			
6	Accum Depr		0		200
7	A/P		6 000		
8	Capital		40000		
9	Drawing	2 000			
10	Fees Inc.		30 925		
11	Adv Exp	1 500			
12	Depr exp	0		200	
13	Ins exp	0		2500	
14	Rent exp	2 600			
15	Salaries exp	6 700			
16	Supplies exp	0		1050	
17	Telephone Exp	350			
18	Utilities exp	850			
19	totals				
20	Net Income				
21					
22					
23					
24					
25					
26					
27					
28					
29					
30					
31					
32					

ADJUSTED TRIAL BALANCE		INCOME STATEMENT		BALANCE SHEET		
DEBIT	CREDIT	DEBIT	CREDIT	DEBIT	CREDIT	
18475				18475		1
3400				3400		2
1100				1100		3
12500				12500		4
24000				24000		5
	200				200	6
	6000				6000	7
	40000				40000	8
2000				2000		9
	30925		30925			10
1500		1500				11
200		200				12
2500		2500				13
2500		2500				14
6700		6700				15
1050		1050				16
350		350				17
850		850				18
77125	77125	15650	30925	61475	46200	19
		5275			15275	20

CHAPTER 5 CHALLENGE PROBLEM (continued)

CHAPTER 5 CHALLENGE PROBLEM (continued)

CHAPTER 5 CHALLENGE PROBLEM (continued)

GENERAL JOURNAL

PAGE _____

	DATE	DESCRIPTION	POST. REF.	DEBIT	CREDIT	
1						1
2						2
3						3
4						4
5						5
6						6
7						7
8						8
9						9
10						10
11						11

GENERAL LEDGER

ACCOUNT _____   ACCOUNT NO. _____

DATE	DESCRIPTION	POST. REF.	DEBIT	CREDIT	BALANCE	
					DEBIT	CREDIT

ACCOUNT _____   ACCOUNT NO. _____

DATE	DESCRIPTION	POST. REF.	DEBIT	CREDIT	BALANCE	
					DEBIT	CREDIT

ACCOUNT _____   ACCOUNT NO. _____

DATE	DESCRIPTION	POST. REF.	DEBIT	CREDIT	BALANCE	
					DEBIT	CREDIT

Name _____

CHAPTER 5 CHALLENGE PROBLEM (continued)

GENERAL LEDGER

ACCOUNT _____ ACCOUNT NO. _____

DATE	DESCRIPTION	POST. REF.	DEBIT	CREDIT	BALANCE	
					DEBIT	CREDIT

ACCOUNT _____ ACCOUNT NO. _____

DATE	DESCRIPTION	POST. REF.	DEBIT	CREDIT	BALANCE	
					DEBIT	CREDIT

ACCOUNT _____ ACCOUNT NO. _____

DATE	DESCRIPTION	POST. REF.	DEBIT	CREDIT	BALANCE	
					DEBIT	CREDIT

Analyze: _____

_____

EXTRA FORMS

ACCOUNT _____ ACCOUNT NO. _____

DATE	DESCRIPTION	POST. REF.	DEBIT	CREDIT	BALANCE	
					DEBIT	CREDIT

ACCOUNT _____ ACCOUNT NO. _____

DATE	DESCRIPTION	POST. REF.	DEBIT	CREDIT	BALANCE	
					DEBIT	CREDIT

CHAPTER 5 CRITICAL THINKING PROBLEM

TO: _____

FROM: _____

DATE: _____

SUBJECT: _____

_____

_____

_____

_____

_____

_____

_____

_____

_____

_____

_____

_____

_____

_____

_____

_____

_____

_____

_____

_____

_____

_____

_____

_____

_____

_____

Chapter 5 Practice Test Answer Key

Part A True-False		Part B Matching	
1. T	6. T	1. a	4. c
2. F	7. T	2. e	5. b
3. T	8. T	3. f	6. d
4. T	9. F		
5. T	10. T		

CHAPTER 6

Closing Entries and the Postclosing Trial Balance

STUDY GUIDE

Understanding the Chapter

Objectives	**1.** Journalize and post closing entries. **2.** Prepare a postclosing trial balance. **3.** Interpret financial statements. **4.** Review the steps in the accounting cycle. **5.** Define the accounting terms new to this chapter.
Reading Assignment	Read Chapter 6 in the textbook. Complete the textbook Section Self Review as you finish reading each section of the chapter, and the Comprehensive Self Review at the end of the chapter. Refer to the Chapter 6 Glossary or to the Glossary at the end of the book to find definitions for terms that are not familiar to you.

Activities

❑ **Thinking Critically** — Answer the *Thinking Critically* questions for Carnival Corporation, Accounting on the Job, and Managerial Implications.

❑ **Internet Application** — Complete the activity for Accounting on the Job.

❑ **Discussion Questions** — Answer each assigned discussion question in Chapter 6.

❑ **Exercises** — Complete each assigned exercise in Chapter 6. Use the forms provided in this SGWP. The objectives covered by an exercise are given after the exercise number. If you need help with an exercise, review the portion of the chapter related to the objective(s) covered.

❑ **Problems A/B** — Complete each assigned problem in Chapter 6. Use the forms provided in this SGWP. The objectives covered by a problem are given after the problem number. If you need help with a problem, review the portion of the chapter related to the objective(s) covered.

❑ **Challenge Problem** — Complete the challenge problem as assigned. Use the forms provided in this SGWP.

❑ **Critical Thinking Problem** — Complete the critical thinking problem as assigned. Use the forms provided in this SGWP.

❑ **Business Connections** — Complete the Business Connections activities as assigned to gain a deeper understanding of Chapter 6 concepts.

Practice Tests

Complete the Practice Tests, which cover the main points in your reading assignment. Compare your answers with those in the Practice Test Answer Key for Chapter 6 at the end of this chapter. If you have answered any questions incorrectly, review the related section of the text.

Part A True-False   *For each of the following statements, circle T in the answer column if the statement is true or F if the statement is false.*

T   F   **1.** The general ledger is a continuing record.

T   F   **2.** The postclosing trial balance will show figures for asset, liability, owner's equity, revenue, and expense accounts.

T   F   **3.** The total of all expenses appears on the credit side of the **Income Summary** account.

T   F   **4.** To close a revenue account, the accountant debits that account and credits the **Income Summary** account.

T   F   **5.** All asset accounts are closed into the **Income Summary** account.

T   F   **6.** The balance of the **Income Summary** account—net income or net loss—is transferred to the owner's capital account.

T   F   **7.** The Income Summary is a financial statement prepared at the end of each accounting period.

T   F   **8.** Adjusting entries create a permanent record of any changes in account balances that are shown on the worksheet.

T   F   **9.** If an adjustment is not made for supplies used, the net income for the period will be understated.

T   F   **10.** Closing entries reduce the balance of revenue and asset accounts to zero so that they are ready to receive data for the next period.

Part B Matching   *For each numbered item, choose the matching term from the box and write the identifying letter in the answer column.*

_____   **1.** The procedure of journalizing and posting the results of operations at the end of an accounting period.

_____   **2.** Journal entries used to transfer the balances of the revenue and expense accounts to the summary accounts as part of the end-of-period procedures.

_____   **3.** Special account in the general ledger used for combining data about revenue and expenses.

_____   **4.** Term used when referring to an account after its balance has been transferred out.

_____   **5.** The last step in the end-of-period procedure, which shows the accountant that it is safe to proceed with entries for the new period.

> **a.** Closing the accounting records
> **b.** Closing entries
> **c.** Closed account
> **d.** Postclosing trial balance
> **e.** Income Summary

Demonstration Problem

The Income Statement and Balance Sheet sections of the worksheet for George Burke for the period ended December 31, 2007 are shown below.

Instructions

1. Journalize the closing entries on page 24 of a general journal.

2. Determine the new balance for Capital once the closing entries have been posted.

George Burke

Worksheet

Month Ended December 31, 2007

	ACCOUNT NAME	INCOME STATEMENT DEBIT	INCOME STATEMENT CREDIT	BALANCE SHEET DEBIT	BALANCE SHEET CREDIT
1	Cash			96 0 0 0 00	
2	Accounts Receivable			6 0 0 0 00	
3	Supplies			12 0 0 0 00	
4	Prepaid Rent			9 0 0 0 00	
5	Equipment			60 0 0 0 00	
6	Accumulated Depreciation—Equipment				1 4 4 0 00
7	Accounts Payable				15 0 0 0 00
8	George Burke, Capital				109 5 0 0 00
9	George Burke, Drawing			6 0 0 0 00	
10	Fees Income		90 0 0 0 00		
11	Salaries Expense	14 4 0 0 00			
12	Utilities Expense	2 1 0 0 00			
13	Supplies Expense	4 8 0 0 00			
14	Advertising Expense	4 2 0 0 00			
15	Depreciation Expense—Equipment	1 4 4 0 00			
16	Totals	26 9 4 0 00	90 0 0 0 00	189 0 0 0 00	125 9 4 0 00
17	Net Income	63 0 6 0 00			63 0 6 0 00
18		90 0 0 0 00	90 0 0 0 00	189 0 0 0 00	189 0 0 0 00
19					

SOLUTION

	DATE		DESCRIPTION	POST. REF.	DEBIT	CREDIT	
1			**Closing Entries**				1
2	2007						2
3	Dec.	31	Fees Income	401	90 0 0 0 00		3
4			Income Summary	399		90 0 0 0 00	4
5							5
6		31	Income Summary	399	26 9 4 0 00		6
7			Salaries Expense	511		14 4 0 0 00	7
8			Utilities Expense	514		2 1 0 0 00	8
9			Supplies Expense	517		4 8 0 0 00	9
10			Advertising Expense	522		4 2 0 0 00	10
11			Depreciation Expense—Equipment	523		1 4 4 0 00	11
12							12
13		31	Income Summary	399	63 0 6 0 00		13
14			George Burke, Capital	301		63 0 6 0 00	14
15							15
16		31	George Burke, Capital	301	6 0 0 0 00		16
17			George Burke, Drawing	302		6 0 0 0 00	17
18							18

New Capital Balance:

George Burke, Capital, December 1, 2007		$109,500.00
Add: Net Income	63,060.00	
Less Withdrawals for December	(6,000.00)	
Increase in Capital		57,060.00
George Burke, Capital, December 31, 2007		$166,560.00

WORKING PAPERS

EXERCISE 6.1

GENERAL JOURNAL   PAGE _____

	DATE		DESCRIPTION	POST. REF.	DEBIT	CREDIT	
1	Dec		Fees Income		85000		1
2			Income Summary			85000	2
3							3
4							4
5							5
6							6
7							7
8							8
9							9
10							10
11							11
12							12
13							13
14							14
15							15
16							16
17							17
18							18
19							19
20							20
21							21

EXERCISE 6.2

1. _____
2. _____
3. _____
4. _____
5. _____
6. _____
7. _____
8. _____
9. _____

EXERCISE 6.3

1. _____   5. _____
2. _____   6. _____
3. _____   7. _____
4. _____

EXERCISE 6.4

1. _____   6. _____   11. _____
2. _____   7. _____   12. _____
3. _____   8. _____   13. _____
4. _____   9. _____   14. _____
5. _____   10. _____   15. _____

EXERCISE 6.5

1. Total revenue for the period is _____ .

2. Total expenses for the period are _____ .

3. Net income for the period is _____ .

4. Owner's withdrawals for the period are _____ .

EXERCISE 6.6

GENERAL JOURNAL   PAGE _____

	DATE	DESCRIPTION	POST. REF.	DEBIT	CREDIT	
1						1
2						2
3						3
4						4
5						5
6						6
7						7
8						8
9						9
10						10
11						11
12						12
13						13
14						14
15						15
16						16
17						17
18						18
19						19
20						20
21						21
22						22
23						23
24						24
25						25
26						26
27						27
28						28
29						29
30						30
31						31
32						32
33						33
34						34
35						35
36						36
37						37

EXERCISE 6.6 (continued)

GENERAL LEDGER

ACCOUNT __Dennis Ortiz, Capital_____ ACCOUNT NO. ____301____

DATE		DESCRIPTION	POST. REF.	DEBIT	CREDIT	BALANCE	
						DEBIT	CREDIT
2007							
Mar.	31	Balance	✔				58 8 0 0 00

ACCOUNT __Dennis Ortiz, Drawing_____ ACCOUNT NO. ____302____

DATE		DESCRIPTION	POST. REF.	DEBIT	CREDIT	BALANCE	
						DEBIT	CREDIT
2007							
Mar.	31	Balance	✔			3 0 0 0 00	

ACCOUNT __Income Summary_____ ACCOUNT NO. ____399____

DATE	DESCRIPTION	POST. REF.	DEBIT	CREDIT	BALANCE	
					DEBIT	CREDIT

ACCOUNT __Fees Income_____ ACCOUNT NO. ____401____

DATE		DESCRIPTION	POST. REF.	DEBIT	CREDIT	BALANCE	
						DEBIT	CREDIT
2007							
Mar.	31	Balance	✔				138 0 0 0 00

ACCOUNT __Depreciation Expense—Equipment_____ ACCOUNT NO. ____510____

DATE		DESCRIPTION	POST. REF.	DEBIT	CREDIT	BALANCE	
						DEBIT	CREDIT
2007							
Mar.	31	Balance	✔			5 0 4 0 00	

EXERCISE 6.6 (continued)

GENERAL LEDGER

ACCOUNT __Insurance Expense__   ACCOUNT NO. ___511___

DATE		DESCRIPTION	POST. REF.	DEBIT	CREDIT	BALANCE DEBIT	BALANCE CREDIT
2007							
Mar.	31	Balance	✔			4 8 0 0 00	

ACCOUNT __Rent Expense__   ACCOUNT NO. ___514___

DATE		DESCRIPTION	POST. REF.	DEBIT	CREDIT	BALANCE DEBIT	BALANCE CREDIT
2007							
Mar.	31	Balance	✔			14 4 0 0 00	

ACCOUNT __Salaries Expense__   ACCOUNT NO. ___517___

DATE		DESCRIPTION	POST. REF.	DEBIT	CREDIT	BALANCE DEBIT	BALANCE CREDIT
2007							
Mar.	31	Balance	✔			70 8 0 0 00	

ACCOUNT __Supplies Expense__   ACCOUNT NO. ___518___

DATE		DESCRIPTION	POST. REF.	DEBIT	CREDIT	BALANCE DEBIT	BALANCE CREDIT
2007							
Mar.	31	Balance	✔			1 9 5 0 00	

ACCOUNT __Telephone Expense__   ACCOUNT NO. ___519___

DATE		DESCRIPTION	POST. REF.	DEBIT	CREDIT	BALANCE DEBIT	BALANCE CREDIT
2007							
Mar.	31	Balance	✔			2 7 0 0 00	

Name _____

EXERCISE 6.6 (continued)

GENERAL LEDGER

ACCOUNT _Utilities Expense_ _____ ACCOUNT NO. ___523___

DATE		DESCRIPTION	POST. REF.	DEBIT	CREDIT	BALANCE	
						DEBIT	CREDIT
2007							
Mar.	31	Balance	✔			3 6 0 0 00	

EXTRA FORMS

ACCOUNT _____ ACCOUNT NO. _____

DATE		DESCRIPTION	POST. REF.	DEBIT	CREDIT	BALANCE	
						DEBIT	CREDIT

ACCOUNT _____ ACCOUNT NO. _____

DATE		DESCRIPTION	POST. REF.	DEBIT	CREDIT	BALANCE	
						DEBIT	CREDIT

ACCOUNT _____ ACCOUNT NO. _____

DATE		DESCRIPTION	POST. REF.	DEBIT	CREDIT	BALANCE	
						DEBIT	CREDIT

112 ■ Chapter 6

EXERCISE 6.7

GENERAL JOURNAL   PAGE _____

	DATE		DESCRIPTION	POST. REF.	DEBIT	CREDIT	
1							1
2							2
3							3
4							4
5							5
6							6
7							7
8							8

_____

_____

EXERCISE 6.8

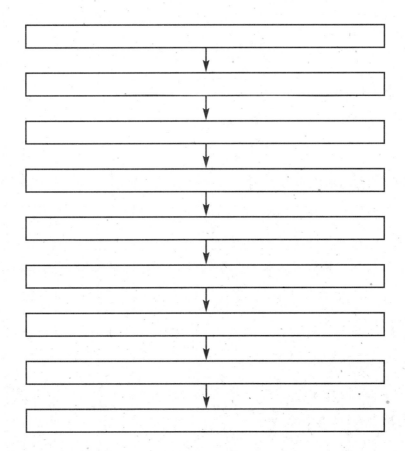

PROBLEM 6.1A or 6.1B

GENERAL JOURNAL   PAGE _____

	DATE		DESCRIPTION	POST. REF.	DEBIT	CREDIT	
1							1
2							2
3							3
4							4
5							5
6							6
7							7
8							8
9							9
10							10
11							11

GENERAL JOURNAL   PAGE _____

	DATE		DESCRIPTION	POST. REF.	DEBIT	CREDIT	
1							1
2							2
3							3
4							4
5							5
6							6
7							7
8							8
9							9
10							10
11							11
12							12
13							13
14							14
15							15
16							16
17							17
18							18
19							19
20							20

Analyze: _____

PROBLEM 6.2A or 6.2B

GENERAL JOURNAL

PAGE _____

	DATE		DESCRIPTION	POST. REF.	DEBIT	CREDIT	
1							1
2							2
3							3
4							4
5							5
6							6
7							7
8							8
9							9
10							10
11							11

GENERAL JOURNAL

PAGE _____

	DATE		DESCRIPTION	POST. REF.	DEBIT	CREDIT	
1							1
2							2
3							3
4							4
5							5
6							6
7							7
8							8
9							9
10							10
11							11
12							12
13							13
14							14
15							15
16							16
17							17
18							18

PROBLEM 6.2A or 6.2B (continued)

GENERAL LEDGER

ACCOUNT **Supplies**   ACCOUNT NO. **121**

DATE	DESCRIPTION	POST. REF.	DEBIT	CREDIT	BALANCE	
					DEBIT	CREDIT

ACCOUNT **Prepaid Advertising**   ACCOUNT NO. **131**

DATE	DESCRIPTION	POST. REF.	DEBIT	CREDIT	BALANCE	
					DEBIT	CREDIT

ACCOUNT **Accumulated Depreciation—Equipment**   ACCOUNT NO. **142**

DATE	DESCRIPTION	POST. REF.	DEBIT	CREDIT	BALANCE	
					DEBIT	CREDIT

ACCOUNT **Capital**   ACCOUNT NO. **301**

DATE	DESCRIPTION	POST. REF.	DEBIT	CREDIT	BALANCE	
					DEBIT	CREDIT

ACCOUNT **Drawing**   ACCOUNT NO. **302**

DATE	DESCRIPTION	POST. REF.	DEBIT	CREDIT	BALANCE	
					DEBIT	CREDIT

PROBLEM 6.2A or 6.2B (continued)

GENERAL LEDGER

ACCOUNT __Income Summary_____ ACCOUNT NO. ___399___

DATE	DESCRIPTION	POST. REF.	DEBIT	CREDIT	BALANCE	
					DEBIT	CREDIT

ACCOUNT __Fees Income_____ ACCOUNT NO. ___401___

DATE	DESCRIPTION	POST. REF.	DEBIT	CREDIT	BALANCE	
					DEBIT	CREDIT

GENERAL LEDGER

ACCOUNT __Salaries Expense_____ ACCOUNT NO. ___511___

DATE	DESCRIPTION	POST. REF.	DEBIT	CREDIT	BALANCE	
					DEBIT	CREDIT

ACCOUNT __Utilities Expense_____ ACCOUNT NO. ___514___

DATE	DESCRIPTION	POST. REF.	DEBIT	CREDIT	BALANCE	
					DEBIT	CREDIT

ACCOUNT __Supplies Expense_____ ACCOUNT NO. ___517___

DATE	DESCRIPTION	POST. REF.	DEBIT	CREDIT	BALANCE	
					DEBIT	CREDIT

PROBLEM 6.2A or 6.2B (continued)

ACCOUNT __Advertising Expense_____ ACCOUNT NO. ____526____

DATE	DESCRIPTION	POST. REF.	DEBIT	CREDIT	BALANCE	
					DEBIT	CREDIT

ACCOUNT __Depreciation Expense—Equipment_____ ACCOUNT NO. ____523____

DATE	DESCRIPTION	POST. REF.	DEBIT	CREDIT	BALANCE	
					DEBIT	CREDIT

ACCOUNT NAME	DEBIT	CREDIT

Analyze: _____

_____

PROBLEM 6.3A or 6.3B

GENERAL JOURNAL

PAGE _____

	DATE	DESCRIPTION	POST. REF.	DEBIT	CREDIT	
1						1
2						2
3						3
4						4
5						5
6						6
7						7
8						8
9						9
10						10
11						11
12						12
13						13
14						14
15						15
16						16
17						17
18						18
19						19
20						20
21						21
22						22
23						23
24						24
25						25
26						26
27						27
28						28
29						29
30						30
31						31
32						32
33						33
34						34
35						35
36						36
37						37

PROBLEM 6.3A or 6.3B (continued)

GENERAL LEDGER

ACCOUNT _____**Capital**_____ ACCOUNT NO. ____**301**____

DATE	DESCRIPTION	POST. REF.	DEBIT	CREDIT	BALANCE	
					DEBIT	CREDIT

ACCOUNT _____**Drawing**_____ ACCOUNT NO. ____**302**____

DATE	DESCRIPTION	POST. REF.	DEBIT	CREDIT	BALANCE	
					DEBIT	CREDIT

ACCOUNT __**Income Summary**_____ ACCOUNT NO. ____**399**____

DATE	DESCRIPTION	POST. REF.	DEBIT	CREDIT	BALANCE	
					DEBIT	CREDIT

ACCOUNT __**Fees Income**_____ ACCOUNT NO. ____**401**____

DATE	DESCRIPTION	POST. REF.	DEBIT	CREDIT	BALANCE	
					DEBIT	CREDIT

PROBLEM 6.3A or 6.3B (continued)

GENERAL LEDGER

ACCOUNT __Advertising Expense__   ACCOUNT NO. __511__

DATE	DESCRIPTION	POST. REF.	DEBIT	CREDIT	BALANCE DEBIT	CREDIT

ACCOUNT __Depreciation Expense—Equipment__   ACCOUNT NO. __514__

DATE	DESCRIPTION	POST. REF.	DEBIT	CREDIT	BALANCE DEBIT	CREDIT

ACCOUNT __Rent Expense__   ACCOUNT NO. __517__

DATE	DESCRIPTION	POST. REF.	DEBIT	CREDIT	BALANCE DEBIT	CREDIT

ACCOUNT __Salaries Expense__   ACCOUNT NO. __519__

DATE	DESCRIPTION	POST. REF.	DEBIT	CREDIT	BALANCE DEBIT	CREDIT

ACCOUNT __Utilities Expense__   ACCOUNT NO. __523__

DATE	DESCRIPTION	POST. REF.	DEBIT	CREDIT	BALANCE DEBIT	CREDIT

Analyze: _____

PROBLEM 6.3A or 6.3B (continued)

GENERAL LEDGER

ACCOUNT _____ ACCOUNT NO. _____

DATE	DESCRIPTION	POST. REF.	DEBIT	CREDIT	BALANCE	
					DEBIT	CREDIT

ACCOUNT _____ ACCOUNT NO. _____

DATE	DESCRIPTION	POST. REF.	DEBIT	CREDIT	BALANCE	
					DEBIT	CREDIT

ACCOUNT _____ ACCOUNT NO. _____

DATE	DESCRIPTION	POST. REF.	DEBIT	CREDIT	BALANCE	
					DEBIT	CREDIT

ACCOUNT _____ ACCOUNT NO. _____

DATE	DESCRIPTION	POST. REF.	DEBIT	CREDIT	BALANCE	
					DEBIT	CREDIT

ACCOUNT _____ ACCOUNT NO. _____

DATE	DESCRIPTION	POST. REF.	DEBIT	CREDIT	BALANCE	
					DEBIT	CREDIT

PROBLEM 6.3A or 6.3B (continued)

GENERAL LEDGER

ACCOUNT _____ ACCOUNT NO. _____

DATE	DESCRIPTION	POST. REF.	DEBIT	CREDIT	BALANCE	
					DEBIT	CREDIT

ACCOUNT _____ ACCOUNT NO. _____

DATE	DESCRIPTION	POST. REF.	DEBIT	CREDIT	BALANCE	
					DEBIT	CREDIT

ACCOUNT _____ ACCOUNT NO. _____

DATE	DESCRIPTION	POST. REF.	DEBIT	CREDIT	BALANCE	
					DEBIT	CREDIT

ACCOUNT _____ ACCOUNT NO. _____

DATE	DESCRIPTION	POST. REF.	DEBIT	CREDIT	BALANCE	
					DEBIT	CREDIT

ACCOUNT _____ ACCOUNT NO. _____

DATE	DESCRIPTION	POST. REF.	DEBIT	CREDIT	BALANCE	
					DEBIT	CREDIT

PROBLEM 6.4A or 6.4B

_____

	ACCOUNT NAME	TRIAL BALANCE		ADJUSTMENTS	
		DEBIT	CREDIT	DEBIT	CREDIT
1	Cash	62100			
2	A/R	9900			
3	Supplies	5000			3200
4	Prepaid Advertising	6000			2800
5	Equipment	40000			
6	Accumulated Depre				960
7	A/P		10000		
8	Capital		71000		
9	Drawing	4000			
10	Fees Income		60000		
11	Salaries Expense	9660			
12	Utilities Expense	1400			
13	Supplies Expense			3200	
14	Advertising Expense			2800	
15	Depreciation Expense			960	
16	Totals	141000	141000	6960	6960
17					
18					
19					
20					
21					
22					
23					
24					
25					
26					
27					
28					
29					
30					
31					
32					

PROBLEM 6.4A or 6.4B (continued)

ADJUSTED TRIAL BALANCE		INCOME STATEMENT		BALANCE SHEET		
DEBIT	CREDIT	DEBIT	CREDIT	DEBIT	CREDIT	
62100				62100		1
9900				9900		2
4800				4800		3
3200				3200		4
40000				40000		5
	960				960	6
	10000				10000	7
	71000				71000	8
4000				4000		9
	60000		60000			10
9600		9600				11
1400		1400				12
3200		3200				13
2800		2800				14
960		960				15
141960	141960	17960	60000	124000	81960	16
		42040	42040		42000	17
					42040	18
						19
						20
						21
						22
						23
						24
						25
						26
						27
						28
						29
						30
						31
						32

PROBLEM 6.4A or 6.4B (continued)

GENERAL JOURNAL

PAGE _____

	DATE	DESCRIPTION	POST. REF.	DEBIT	CREDIT	
1		Supplies Expense		3200		1
2		Supplies			3200	2
3		Advertising Expense		2800		3
4		Prepaid Advertising			2800	4
5		Depreciation Expense		960		5
6		Accumulated Depreciation			960	6
7						7
8						8
9						9
10						10
11						11
12						12
13						13

GENERAL JOURNAL

PAGE _____

	DATE	DESCRIPTION	POST. REF.	DEBIT	CREDIT	
1		Fees Income		60000		1
2		Income Summary			60000	2
3		Income Summary		17960		3
4		Supplies Expense			3200	4
5		Advertising Expense			2800	5
6		Depreciation Expense			960	6
7		Salaries Expense			9600	7
8		Utilities Expense			1400	8
9		Income Summary		42040		9
10		Capital			42040	10
11		Capital		4000		11
12		Drawing			4000	12
13						13
14						14
15						15
16						16
17						17
18						18

PROBLEM 6.4A or 6.4B (continued)

GENERAL LEDGER

ACCOUNT __Supplies__   ACCOUNT NO. ___121___

DATE	DESCRIPTION	POST. REF.	DEBIT	CREDIT	BALANCE DEBIT	BALANCE CREDIT
					8000	
	Adj			3200	4800	

ACCOUNT __Prepaid Advertising__   ACCOUNT NO. ___131___

DATE	DESCRIPTION	POST. REF.	DEBIT	CREDIT	BALANCE DEBIT	BALANCE CREDIT
					6000	
	Adj			2800	3200	

ACCOUNT __Accumulated Depreciation—__   ACCOUNT NO. ___142___

DATE	DESCRIPTION	POST. REF.	DEBIT	CREDIT	BALANCE DEBIT	BALANCE CREDIT
						960

ACCOUNT __Capital__   ACCOUNT NO. ___301___

DATE	DESCRIPTION	POST. REF.	DEBIT	CREDIT	BALANCE DEBIT	BALANCE CREDIT
						71000
				42040		113040
			4000			109040

ACCOUNT __Drawing__   ACCOUNT NO. ___302___

DATE	DESCRIPTION	POST. REF.	DEBIT	CREDIT	BALANCE DEBIT	BALANCE CREDIT
					4000	
				4000	0	

PROBLEM 6.4A or 6.4B (continued)

GENERAL LEDGER

ACCOUNT __Income Summary__   ACCOUNT NO. ___399___

DATE	DESCRIPTION	POST. REF.	DEBIT	CREDIT	BALANCE DEBIT	BALANCE CREDIT
						60000
			17960			42040
			42040			0

ACCOUNT __Fees Income__   ACCOUNT NO. ___401___

DATE	DESCRIPTION	POST. REF.	DEBIT	CREDIT	BALANCE DEBIT	BALANCE CREDIT
	Balance			60000		60000
	Closing		60000			0

GENERAL LEDGER

ACCOUNT __Salaries Expense__   ACCOUNT NO. ___511___

DATE	DESCRIPTION	POST. REF.	DEBIT	CREDIT	BALANCE DEBIT	BALANCE CREDIT
					9600	
	Closing			9600	0	

ACCOUNT __Utilities Expense__   ACCOUNT NO. ___514___

DATE	DESCRIPTION	POST. REF.	DEBIT	CREDIT	BALANCE DEBIT	BALANCE CREDIT
	Closing			1400	1400	
					0	

ACCOUNT __Supplies Expense__   ACCOUNT NO. ___517___

DATE	DESCRIPTION	POST. REF.	DEBIT	CREDIT	BALANCE DEBIT	BALANCE CREDIT
	Adj.		3200		3200	
	Closing			3200	0	

PROBLEM 6.4A or 6.4B (continued)

ACCOUNT __Advertising Expense_____ ACCOUNT NO. ___526___

DATE	DESCRIPTION	POST. REF.	DEBIT	CREDIT	BALANCE DEBIT	BALANCE CREDIT
					2800	
	Closing			2800	0	

ACCOUNT __Depreciation Expense—_____ ACCOUNT NO. ___523___

DATE	DESCRIPTION	POST. REF.	DEBIT	CREDIT	BALANCE DEBIT	BALANCE CREDIT
					960	
	Closing			960	0	

ACCOUNT NAME	DEBIT	CREDIT

Analyze: _____

CHAPTER 6 CHALLENGE PROBLEM

The Barber Shop

Worksheet

Month Ended December 31, 2007

	ACCOUNT NAME	TRIAL BALANCE DEBIT	TRIAL BALANCE CREDIT	ADJUSTMENTS DEBIT	ADJUSTMENTS CREDIT
1	Cash	40 8 0 0 00			
2	Accounts Receivable	9 0 0 0 00			
3	Supplies	7 2 0 0 00			(a) 3 6 0 0 00
4	Prepaid Insurance	10 8 0 0 00			(b) 2 4 0 0 00
5	Machinery	84 0 0 0 00			
6	Accumulated Depreciation—Machinery				(c) 1 2 0 0 00
7	Accounts Payable		13 5 0 0 00		
8	Tommy Brooks, Capital		74 5 8 0 00		
9	Tommy Brooks, Drawing	6 0 0 0 00			
10	Fees Income		82 5 0 0 00		
11	Supplies Expense			(a) 3 6 0 0 00	
12	Insurance Expense			(b) 2 4 0 0 00	
13	Salaries Expense	11 1 0 0 00			
14	Depreciation Expense—Machinery			(c) 1 2 0 0 00	
15	Utilities Expense	1 6 8 0 00			
16	Totals	170 5 8 0 00	170 5 8 0 00	7 2 0 0 00	7 2 0 0 00
17	Net Income				
18					
19					
20					
21					
22					
23					
24					
25					
26					
27					
28					
29					
30					
31					
32					

Name _____

CHAPTER 6 CHALLENGE PROBLEM (continued)

_____

ADJUSTED TRIAL BALANCE		INCOME STATEMENT		BALANCE SHEET		
DEBIT	CREDIT	DEBIT	CREDIT	DEBIT	CREDIT	
						1
						2
						3
						4
						5
						6
						7
						8
						9
						10
						11
						12
						13
						14
						15
						16
						17
						18
						19
						20
						21
						22
						23
						24
						25
						26
						27
						28
						29
						30
						31
						32

CHAPTER 6 CHALLENGE PROBLEM (continued)

CHAPTER 6 CHALLENGE PROBLEM (continued)

GENERAL JOURNAL   PAGE _____

	DATE		DESCRIPTION	POST. REF.	DEBIT	CREDIT	
1							1
2							2
3							3
4							4
5							5
6							6
7							7
8							8
9							9
10							10
11							11
12							12
13							13
14							14
15							15
16							16

CHAPTER 6 CHALLENGE PROBLEM (continued)

GENERAL JOURNAL   PAGE _____

	DATE		DESCRIPTION	POST. REF.	DEBIT	CREDIT	
1							1
2							2
3							3
4							4
5							5
6							6
7							7
8							8
9							9
10							10
11							11
12							12
13							13
14							14
15							15
16							16
17							17
18							18

ACCOUNT NAME	DEBIT	CREDIT

Analyze: _____

CHAPTER 6 CRITICAL THINKING PROBLEM

1. _____

_____

_____

_____

_____

_____

_____

_____

_____

2.

GENERAL JOURNAL   PAGE _____

	DATE		DESCRIPTION	POST. REF.	DEBIT	CREDIT	
1							1
2							2
3							3
4							4
5							5
6							6

3. _____

_____

_____

_____

_____

_____

_____

_____

_____

_____

_____

_____

_____

_____

CHAPTER 6 CRITICAL THINKING PROBLEM (continued)

_____

_____

_____

_____

_____

_____

_____

_____

_____

_____

_____

_____

_____

_____

_____

_____

_____

_____

_____

_____

Chapter 6 Practice Test Answer Key

Part A True-False	Part B Matching
1. T	1. a
2. F	2. b
3. F	3. e
4. T	4. c
5. F	5. d
6. T	
7. F	
8. T	
9. F	
10. F	

CHAPTER 7

Accounting for Sales and Accounts Receivable

STUDY GUIDE

Understanding the Chapter

Objectives	**1.** Record credit sales in a sales journal. **2.** Post from the sales journal to the general ledger accounts. **3.** Post from the sales journal to the customers' accounts in the accounts receivable subsidiary ledger. **4.** Record sales returns and allowances in the general journal. **5.** Post sales returns and allowances. **6.** Prepare a schedule of accounts receivable. **7.** Compute trade discounts. **8.** Record credit card sales in appropriate journals. **9.** Prepare the state sales tax return. **10.** Define the accounting terms new to this chapter.
Reading Assignment	Read Chapter 7 in the textbook. Complete the textbook Section Self Review as you finish reading each section of the chapter, and the Comprehensive Self Review at the end of the chapter. Refer to the Chapter 7 Glossary or to the Glossary at the end of the book to find definitions for terms that are not familiar to you.

Activities

❏ **Thinking Critically**	Answer the *Thinking Critically* questions for Wal-Mart, Computers in Accounting, and Managerial Implications.
❏ **Internet Application**	Complete the activity for Computers in Accounting.
❏ **Discussion Questions**	Answer each assigned discussion question in Chapter 7.
❏ **Exercises**	Complete each assigned exercise in Chapter 7. Use the forms provided in this SGWP. The objectives covered by an exercise are given after the exercise number. If you need help with an exercise, review the portion of the chapter related to the objective(s) covered.
❏ **Problems A/B**	Complete each assigned problem in Chapter 7. Use the forms provided in this SGWP. The objectives covered by a problem are given after the problem number. If you need help with a problem, review the portion of the chapter related to the objective(s) covered.
❏ **Challenge Problem**	Complete the challenge problem as assigned. Use the forms provided in this SGWP.
❏ **Critical Thinking Problem**	Complete the critical thinking problem as assigned. Use the forms provided in this SGWP.
❏ **Business Connections**	Complete the Business Connections activities as assigned to gain a deeper understanding of Chapter 7 concepts.

Practice Tests

Complete the Practice Tests, which cover the main points in your reading assignment. Compare your answers with those in the Practice Test Answer Key for Chapter 7 at the end of this chapter. If you have answered any questions incorrectly, review the related section of the text.

Part A True-False *For each of the following statements, circle T in the answer column if the statement is true and F if the statement is false.*

T F **1.** The amount of a sales allowance is debited to the Sales account because the revenue from sales has been reduced.

T F **2.** The larger the volume of credit sales, the more desirable it is to use a special sales journal.

T F **3.** The use of a special sales journal enables more than one person to work on the journals of a business at the same time.

T F **4.** The Sales Slip Number column in the sales journal shows where to look when more information is needed.

T F **5.** The use of a special sales journal makes posting to accounts in the general ledger unnecessary.

T F **6.** The columns and headings in the sales journal eliminate the need for a description of each entity.

T F **7.** The special sales journal is used for recording both cash sales and sales on credit.

T F **8.** The Sales account may be credited for a sale only when cash is received.

T F **9.** Sales on credit require debits to **Accounts Receivable.**

T F **10.** Special journals are needed when the transactions of a business include groups of repetitive entries.

T F **11.** A credit sale made on a credit card issued by a credit card company is accounted for in the same manner as a credit sale made on a bank credit card.

T F **12.** The accountant must keep an individual record of dealings with each customer to answer questions received from managers and salespeople of the company, from the customers themselves, and from banks and credit bureaus.

T F **13.** As proof of accuracy, the total of all customers' accounts in the accounts receivable ledger is compared with the balance of the **Accounts Receivable** account in the general ledger.

T F **14.** The **Accounts Receivable** account in the general ledger is known as a control account because it contains a summary of all activities involving accounts receivable.

T F **15.** When the balance-form ledger sheet is used in the accounts receivable ledger, the accountant figures the running balance of each account after each posting during the month.

T F **16.** The basic procedure for posting totals from the sales journal to the general ledger is not affected by the use of an accounts receivable ledger.

T F **17.** The amount of each credit sale is posted daily to the customer's account in the accounts receivable ledger.

T F **18.** The accounts receivable ledger is called a subsidiary ledger because it is only a part of the general ledger.

T F **19.** The **Accounts Receivable** account in the general ledger must be individually debited for each credit sale as it is made.

T F **20.** When a customer returns goods on which sales tax was charged, the firm gives credit for the price of goods and the sales tax.

Part B Matching

For each numbered item, choose the matching term from the box and write the identifying letter in the answer column.

_____ 1. A special journal for recording only the credit sales of a company.

_____ 2. A liability account for recording a tax levied by some states on certain retail sales.

_____ 3. A reduction in the amount charged to a customer who has received defective goods or services.

_____ 4. A reduction in price, based on volume purchased, given by wholesalers to retailers who buy goods for resale.

_____ 5. The type of credit usually given by a business on the basis of the personal knowledge of the customer.

_____ 6. Identification cards given by some businesses to their customers who have established credit.

_____ 7. Identification cards used by some banks to individuals for use in making credit card purchases at participating businesses.

a. Trade discount
b. Sales return or allowance
c. Business credit card
d. Sales tax payable
e. Open-account credit
f. Sales journal
g. Bank credit cards

Part C Exercise

Answer each question about the accounts receivable subsidiary ledger account shown below.

ACCOUNTS RECEIVABLE SUBSIDIARY LEDGER

NAME __Charles O'Brien__   TERMS _____

ADDRESS __1891 Windsor Drive, Dallas, TX 75623-6998__

DATE		DESCRIPTION	POST. REF.	DEBIT	CREDIT	BALANCE DEBIT	BALANCE CREDIT
2007							
Jan.	1	Balance	✔			4 0 0 00	
	4	Sales Slip 101	S1	6 0 00		4 6 0 00	
	7	Sales Slip 167	S1	9 0 00		5 5 0 00	
	17		J1		7 5 00	4 7 5 00	

1. Where did the $400 entry come from?

_____

_____

2. How could you find a complete description of the $60 charge on January 4?

_____

_____

3. What was the probable reason for the $75.00 entry? How can you find out for sure?

_____

_____

Demonstration Problem

Twin City Auto Supply sells tires and auto supplies to retail stores. The firm offers a trade discount of 40 percent on tires and 20 percent on auto supplies. Transactions involving credit sales and sales returns and allowances for the month of April 2007 follow, along with the general ledger accounts used to record these transactions. Account balances shown are for the beginning of April 2007.

Instructions

1. Open the general ledger accounts; enter the balance for **Accounts Receivable**.
   - 111   Accounts Receivable $61,020
   - 401   Sales
   - 451   Sales Returns and Allowances

2. Set up the accounts receivable subsidiary ledger. Open an account for each credit customer and enter the balances as of April 1, 2007. All customers have terms of n/45.
Auto Mart	$14,790
Auto Discount Supply Center	
Jazzy Wheels and Window Tint Center	$42,000
Mike's Car Care Center	$4,230
City Auto Accessories Express	

3. Record the transactions on page 6 of a sales journal and on page 16 of the general journal. (Be sure to enter each sale at its net price.)

4. Post individual entries from the sales journal and the general journal to the appropriate ledger accounts.

5. Total and rule the sales journal as of April 30, 2007.

6. Post from the sales journal to the appropriate general ledger accounts.

7. Prepare a schedule of accounts receivable for April 30, 2007.

8. Compare the total of the schedule of accounts receivable to the balance of the **Accounts Receivable** account. The two should be equal.

DATE	TRANSACTIONS
April 1	Sold tires to Auto Discount Supply Center; issued invoice 6701 with a list price of $37,200.
5	Sold auto supplies to Mike's Car Care Center; issued invoice 6702 with a list price of $50,700.
9	Sold auto supplies to Jazzy Wheels and Window Tint Center; issued invoice 6703 with a list price of $19,800.
14	Sold tires to Auto Mart, issued invoice 6704 with a list price of $49,200.
18	Accepted a return of all auto supplies damaged in shipment to Jazzy Wheels and Window Tint Center; issued Credit Memorandum 251. The original sale was made on Invoice 6703 on April 9.
22	Sold auto supplies to Auto Discount Supply Center; issued Invoice 6705 with a list price of $93,480.
29	Sold tires to Mike's Car Care Center; issued Invoice 6706 with a list price of $82,230.
30	Sold tires to City Auto Accessories Express; issued Invoice 6707 with a list price of $43,230.

SOLUTION

SALES JOURNAL

	DATE		INVOICE NO.	CUSTOMER'S NAME	POST. REF.	ACCOUNTS RECEIVABLE/ DR. SALES CR.	
1	2007						1
2	April	1	6701	Auto Discount Supply Center	✔	22 3 2 0 00	2
3		5	6702	Mike's Car Care Center	✔	40 5 6 0 00	3
4		9	6703	Jazzy Wheels and Window Tint Center	✔	15 8 4 0 00	4
5		14	6704	Auto Mart	✔	29 5 2 0 00	5
6		22	6705	Auto Discount Supply Center	✔	74 7 8 4 00	6
7		29	6706	Mike's Car Care Center	✔	49 3 3 8 00	7
8		30	6707	City Auto Accessories Express	✔	25 9 3 8 00	8
9						258 3 0 0 00	9
10						(1 1 1/4 01)	10
11							11

GENERAL JOURNAL

	DATE		DESCRIPTION	POST. REF.	DEBIT	CREDIT	
1	2007						1
2	April	18	Sales Returns and Allowances	451	15 8 4 0 00		2
3			Accounts Rec./Jazzy Wheels	111 ✔		15 8 4 0 00	3
4			and Window Tint Center				4
5			Accepted return of damaged supplies,				5
6			Credit Memo 251; original sale				6
7			made on Invoice 6703 of April 9				7
8							8

GENERAL LEDGER

ACCOUNT __Accounts Receivable__   ACCOUNT NO. ___111___

DATE		DESCRIPTION	POST. REF.	DEBIT	CREDIT	BALANCE DEBIT	BALANCE CREDIT
2007							
April	1	Balance	✔			61 0 2 0 00	
	18		J16		15 8 4 0 00	45 1 8 0 00	
	30		S6	258 3 0 0 00		303 4 8 0 00	

SOLUTION (continued)

GENERAL LEDGER

ACCOUNT __Sales__   ACCOUNT NO. ___401___

DATE		DESCRIPTION	POST. REF.	DEBIT	CREDIT	BALANCE DEBIT	BALANCE CREDIT
2007							
April	30		S6		258 3 0 0 00	258 3 0 0 00	

ACCOUNT __Sales Returns and Allowances__   ACCOUNT NO. ___451___

DATE		DESCRIPTION	POST. REF.	DEBIT	CREDIT	BALANCE DEBIT	BALANCE CREDIT
2007							
April	18		J16	15 8 4 0 00		15 8 4 0 00	

ACCOUNTS RECEIVABLE SUBSIDIARY LEDGER

NAME __Auto Discount Supply Center__   TERMS ___n/45___

DATE		DESCRIPTION	POST. REF.	DEBIT	CREDIT	BALANCE DEBIT	BALANCE CREDIT
2007							
April	1		S6	22 3 2 0 00		22 3 2 0 00	
	22		S6	74 7 8 4 00		97 1 0 4 00	

NAME __Auto Mart__   TERMS ___n/45___

DATE		DESCRIPTION	POST. REF.	DEBIT	CREDIT	BALANCE DEBIT	BALANCE CREDIT
2007							
April	1	Balance	✔			14 7 9 0 00	
	14		S6	29 5 2 0 00		44 3 1 0 00	

NAME __City Auto Accessories Express__   TERMS ___n/45___

DATE		DESCRIPTION	POST. REF.	DEBIT	CREDIT	BALANCE DEBIT	BALANCE CREDIT
2007							
April	30		S6	25 9 3 8 00		25 9 3 8 00	

SOLUTION (continued)

ACCOUNTS RECEIVABLE SUBSIDIARY LEDGER

NAME __Jazzy Wheels and Window Tint Center__   TERMS ___n/45___

DATE		DESCRIPTION	POST. REF.	DEBIT	CREDIT	BALANCE DEBIT	BALANCE CREDIT
2007							
April	1	Balance	✔			42 0 0 0 00	
	9		S6	15 8 4 0 00		57 8 4 0 00	
	18		J16		15 8 4 0 00	42 0 0 0 00	

NAME __Mike's Car Care Center__   TERMS ___n/45___

DATE		DESCRIPTION	POST. REF.	DEBIT	CREDIT	BALANCE DEBIT	BALANCE CREDIT
2007							
April	1		✔			4 2 3 0 00	
	5		S6	40 5 6 0 00		44 7 9 0 00	
	29		S6	49 3 3 8 00		94 1 2 8 00	

Twin City Auto Supply
Schedule of Accounts Receivable
April 30, 2007

Auto Discount Supply Center	97 1 0 4 00
Auto Mart	44 3 1 0 00
City Auto Accessories Express	25 9 3 8 00
Jazzy Wheels and Window Tint Center	42 0 0 0 00
Mike's Car Care Center	94 1 2 8 00
Total	303 4 8 0 00

WORKING PAPERS

Name _____

EXERCISE 7.1

1. _____   5. _____

2. _____   6. _____

3. _____   7. _____

4. _____   8. _____

EXERCISE 7.2

	Dr.	Cr.			Dr.	Cr.
1.	_____	_____		4.	_____	_____
2.	_____	_____		5.	_____	_____
3.	_____	_____		6.	_____	_____

EXERCISE 7.3

SALES JOURNAL   PAGE _____

	DATE	SALES SLIP NO.	CUSTOMER'S NAME	POST. REF.	ACCOUNTS RECEIVABLE DEBIT	SALES TAX PAYABLE CREDIT	SALES CREDIT	
1	May 1		Roy Anderson		380	30	360	1
2	May 2		John Amos		050	240	240	2
3	May 3		Teresa Wells		216	16	200	3
4					864	64	800	4
5								5

EXERCISE 7.4

GENERAL JOURNAL   PAGE _____

	DATE	DESCRIPTION	POST. REF.	DEBIT	CREDIT	
1	Jun 7	Sales		600		1
2		Sales Tax Payable		48		2
3		A/R			648	3
4	Jun 22	Sales		900		4
5		Sales Tax		72		5
6		A/R			972	6
7						7
8						8
9						9
10						10
11						11
12						12
13						13
14						14
15						15

EXERCISE 7.5

1. _____
2. _____
3. _____
4. _____

EXERCISE 7.6

1. _____
2. _____
3. _____

EXERCISE 7.7

1. _____
2. _____
3. _____

EXERCISE 7.8

GENERAL JOURNAL PAGE _____

	DATE	DESCRIPTION	POST. REF.	DEBIT	CREDIT	
1						1
2						2
3						3
4						4
5						5

EXERCISE 7.9

_____
_____

Balance of Accounts Receivable: _____

EXERCISE 7.10

GENERAL LEDGER

ACCOUNT _____ ACCOUNT NO. _____

	DATE	DESCRIPTION	POST. REF.	DEBIT	CREDIT	BALANCE DEBIT	BALANCE CREDIT

ACCOUNT _____ ACCOUNT NO. _____

	DATE	DESCRIPTION	POST. REF.	DEBIT	CREDIT	BALANCE DEBIT	BALANCE CREDIT

ACCOUNT _____ ACCOUNT NO. _____

	DATE	DESCRIPTION	POST. REF.	DEBIT	CREDIT	BALANCE DEBIT	BALANCE CREDIT

ACCOUNTS RECEIVABLE SUBSIDIARY LEDGER

NAME _____ TERMS _____

	DATE	DESCRIPTION	POST. REF.	DEBIT	CREDIT	BALANCE

NAME _____ TERMS _____

	DATE	DESCRIPTION	POST. REF.	DEBIT	CREDIT	BALANCE

PROBLEM 7.1A or 7.1B

SALES JOURNAL

PAGE _____

	DATE	SALES SLIP NO.	CUSTOMER'S NAME	POST. REF.	ACCOUNTS RECEIVABLE DEBIT	SALES TAX PAYABLE CREDIT	SALES CREDIT	
1	July 1		Bonnie Franklin		918	68	850	1
2	6		Janet Judge		1134	84	1050	2
3	11		Raymond Clay		2908	208	2600	3
4	17		Melissa Gray		972	72	900	4
5	23		Angela Nguyen		540	40	500	5
6	27		Clifton Wallace		1026	76	950	6
7	29		Sally Wei		1404	104	1300	7
8	31		Ken Holt		432	32	400	8
9					9234	684	8550	9
10								10
11								11
12								12

GENERAL LEDGER

ACCOUNT ___Accounts Receivable___   ACCOUNT NO. ___111___

DATE	DESCRIPTION	POST. REF.	DEBIT	CREDIT	BALANCE DEBIT	BALANCE CREDIT
J 1	Balance				31400	
			9234		40634	

ACCOUNT ___Sales Tax Payable___   ACCOUNT NO. ___231___

DATE	DESCRIPTION	POST. REF.	DEBIT	CREDIT	BALANCE DEBIT	BALANCE CREDIT
	Balance				684	

ACCOUNT ___Sales___   ACCOUNT NO. ___401___

DATE	DESCRIPTION	POST. REF.	DEBIT	CREDIT	BALANCE DEBIT	BALANCE CREDIT
	Balance				8550	

Analyze: _____

_____

PROBLEM 7.2A or 7.2B

SALES JOURNAL

PAGE _____

	DATE	SALES SLIP NO.	CUSTOMER'S NAME	POST. REF.	ACCOUNTS RECEIVABLE DEBIT	SALES TAX PAYABLE CREDIT	SALES CREDIT	
1								1
2								2
3								3
4								4
5								5
6								6
7								7
8								8
9								9
10								10
11								11
12								12

GENERAL JOURNAL

PAGE _____

	DATE	DESCRIPTION	POST. REF.	DEBIT	CREDIT	
1						1
2						2
3						3
4						4
5						5
6						6
7						7
8						8
9						9
10						10
11						11
12						12
13						13
14						14
15						15
16						16
17						17
18						18
19						19
20						20
21						21

PROBLEM 7.2A or 7.2B (continued)

GENERAL LEDGER

ACCOUNT _____ ACCOUNT NO. _____

DATE	DESCRIPTION	POST. REF.	DEBIT	CREDIT	BALANCE	
					DEBIT	CREDIT

ACCOUNT _____ ACCOUNT NO. _____

DATE	DESCRIPTION	POST. REF.	DEBIT	CREDIT	BALANCE	
					DEBIT	CREDIT

ACCOUNT _____ ACCOUNT NO. _____

DATE	DESCRIPTION	POST. REF.	DEBIT	CREDIT	BALANCE	
					DEBIT	CREDIT

ACCOUNT _____ ACCOUNT NO. _____

DATE	DESCRIPTION	POST. REF.	DEBIT	CREDIT	BALANCE	
					DEBIT	CREDIT

Name _____

PROBLEM 7.2A or 7.2B (continued)

Analyze: _____

PROBLEM 7.3A or 7.3B

SALES JOURNAL　　　　PAGE 6

	DATE	SALES SLIP NO.	CUSTOMER'S NAME	POST. REF.	ACCOUNTS RECEIVABLE DEBIT	SALES TAX PAYABLE CREDIT	SALES CREDIT	
1	Nov 1		Pauline Judge		1620	120	1500	1
2	Nov 5		Janet Hutchison		2268	168	2100	2
3	Nov 6		Charles Brown		756	56	700	3
4	Nov 10		Lisa Morgan		1836	36	1700	4
5	Nov 14		Dorothy Watts		594	44	550	5
6	Nov 17		Lisa Morgan					6
7	Nov 21		Winnie Wu		6912	256	3200	7
8	Nov 24		Henry Okafor		648	48	600	8
9	Nov 25		Winnie Wu					9
10	Nov 30		Euline Brock		4104	304	3800	10
11					19479	1172	14750	11
12								12

PROBLEM 7.3A or 7.3B (continued)

GENERAL JOURNAL

	DATE	DESCRIPTION	POST. REF.	DEBIT	CREDIT	
1	Nov 17	Sales R/A		150		1
2		Sales Tax Payable		12		2
3		A/R Morgan			162	3
4						4
5	Nov 25	Sales R/A		350		5
6		Sales Tax Payable		28		6
7		A/R Wu			378	7
8						8
9						9
10						10
11						11
12						12
13						13
14						14
15						15

GENERAL LEDGER

ACCOUNT __Accounts Receivable__ ACCOUNT NO. _____

DATE	DESCRIPTION	POST. REF.	DEBIT	CREDIT	BALANCE DEBIT	BALANCE CREDIT
	Balance				19278	
				162	19116	
				378	18738	

ACCOUNT __Sales Tax Payable__ ACCOUNT NO. _____

DATE	DESCRIPTION	POST. REF.	DEBIT	CREDIT	BALANCE DEBIT	BALANCE CREDIT
	Balance					1172
			12			1160
			28			1132

PROBLEM 7.3A or 7.3B (continued)

GENERAL LEDGER

ACCOUNT _____Sales_____ ACCOUNT NO. _____

DATE	DESCRIPTION	POST. REF.	DEBIT	CREDIT	BALANCE	
					DEBIT	CREDIT
	Balance					17750

ACCOUNT _____Sales R/A_____ ACCOUNT NO. _____

DATE	DESCRIPTION	POST. REF.	DEBIT	CREDIT	BALANCE	
					DEBIT	CREDIT
			150			
	Balance		350		500	

ACCOUNTS RECEIVABLE SUBSIDIARY LEDGER

NAME _____P. Judge_____ TERMS _____

DATE	DESCRIPTION	POST. REF.	DEBIT	CREDIT	BALANCE
	A/R		1620	50	1620

NAME _____J. Hutchison_____ TERMS _____

DATE	DESCRIPTION	POST. REF.	DEBIT	CREDIT	BALANCE
			2248		2268

NAME _____Charles Brown_____ TERMS _____

DATE	DESCRIPTION	POST. REF.	DEBIT	CREDIT	BALANCE
			756		756

PROBLEM 7.3A or 7.3B (continued)

ACCOUNTS RECEIVABLE SUBSIDIARY LEDGER

NAME _____Lisa Morgan_____ TERMS _____

	DATE		DESCRIPTION	POST. REF.	DEBIT	CREDIT	BALANCE
					1 836		
						163	674

NAME _____Dorthy Watts_____ TERMS _____

	DATE		DESCRIPTION	POST. REF.	DEBIT	CREDIT	BALANCE
					504		599

NAME _____Winnie Wu_____ TERMS _____

	DATE		DESCRIPTION	POST. REF.	DEBIT	CREDIT	BALANCE
					6012		
						376	637

NAME _____Euline Brack_____ TERMS _____

	DATE		DESCRIPTION	POST. REF.	DEBIT	CREDIT	BALANCE
					4 104		4 104

NAME _____ TERMS _____

	DATE		DESCRIPTION	POST. REF.	DEBIT	CREDIT	BALANCE

NAME _____ TERMS _____

	DATE		DESCRIPTION	POST. REF.	DEBIT	CREDIT	BALANCE

PROBLEM 7.3A or 7.3B (continued)

Schedule of A/R

P. Judge	1620
J. Hutchison	2268
Charles Brown	756
Lisa Morgan	1674
Dorthy Wetts	594
Winnie Vu	6534
Euline Brock	4104

Balance of Accounts Receivable account: _____

Analyze: _____

PROBLEM 7.4A or 7.4B

SALES JOURNAL   PAGE _____

	DATE	INVOICE NO.	CUSTOMER'S NAME	POST. REF.	ACCOUNTS RECEIVABLE DR./ SALES CR.	
1						1
2						2
3						3
4						4
5						5
6						6
7						7
8						8
9						9
10						10
11						11
12						12

PROBLEM 7.4A or 7.4B (continued)

GENERAL JOURNAL   PAGE _____

	DATE	DESCRIPTION	POST. REF.	DEBIT	CREDIT	
1						1
2						2
3						3
4						4
5						5
6						6
7						7
8						8
9						9
10						10
11						11
12						12
13						13

GENERAL LEDGER

ACCOUNT _____   ACCOUNT NO. _____

DATE	DESCRIPTION	POST. REF.	DEBIT	CREDIT	BALANCE DEBIT	BALANCE CREDIT

ACCOUNT _____   ACCOUNT NO. _____

DATE	DESCRIPTION	POST. REF.	DEBIT	CREDIT	BALANCE DEBIT	BALANCE CREDIT

ACCOUNT _____   ACCOUNT NO. _____

DATE	DESCRIPTION	POST. REF.	DEBIT	CREDIT	BALANCE DEBIT	BALANCE CREDIT

PROBLEM 7.4A or 7.4B (continued)

ACCOUNTS RECEIVABLE SUBSIDIARY LEDGER

NAME _____ TERMS _____

	DATE	DESCRIPTION	POST. REF.	DEBIT	CREDIT	BALANCE

NAME _____ TERMS _____

	DATE	DESCRIPTION	POST. REF.	DEBIT	CREDIT	BALANCE

NAME _____ TERMS _____

	DATE	DESCRIPTION	POST. REF.	DEBIT	CREDIT	BALANCE

NAME _____ TERMS _____

	DATE	DESCRIPTION	POST. REF.	DEBIT	CREDIT	BALANCE

NAME _____ TERMS _____

	DATE	DESCRIPTION	POST. REF.	DEBIT	CREDIT	BALANCE

PROBLEM 7.4A or 7.4B (continued)

ACCOUNTS RECEIVABLE SUBSIDIARY LEDGER

NAME _____ TERMS _____

DATE	DESCRIPTION	POST. REF.	DEBIT	CREDIT	BALANCE

Balance of Accounts Receivable account: _____

Analyze: _____

_____

CHAPTER 7 CHALLENGE PROBLEM

SALES JOURNAL   PAGE _____

	DATE	INVOICE NO.	CUSTOMER'S NAME	POST. REF.	ACCOUNTS RECEIVABLE DR./ SALES CR.	
1						1
2						2
3						3
4						4
5						5
6						6
7						7
8						8
9						9
10						10
11						11

Name _____

CHAPTER 7 CHALLENGE PROBLEM (continued)

GENERAL JOURNAL

PAGE _____

	DATE		DESCRIPTION	POST. REF.	DEBIT	CREDIT	
1							1
2							2
3							3
4							4
5							5
6							6
7							7

GENERAL LEDGER

ACCOUNT _____ ACCOUNT NO. _____

DATE	DESCRIPTION	POST. REF.	DEBIT	CREDIT	BALANCE	
					DEBIT	CREDIT

ACCOUNT _____ ACCOUNT NO. _____

DATE	DESCRIPTION	POST. REF.	DEBIT	CREDIT	BALANCE	
					DEBIT	CREDIT

ACCOUNT _____ ACCOUNT NO. _____

DATE	DESCRIPTION	POST. REF.	DEBIT	CREDIT	BALANCE	
					DEBIT	CREDIT

CHAPTER 7 CHALLENGE PROBLEM (continued)

ACCOUNTS RECEIVABLE SUBSIDIARY LEDGER

NAME _____ TERMS _____

DATE	DESCRIPTION	POST. REF.	DEBIT	CREDIT	BALANCE

NAME _____ TERMS _____

DATE	DESCRIPTION	POST. REF.	DEBIT	CREDIT	BALANCE

NAME _____ TERMS _____

DATE	DESCRIPTION	POST. REF.	DEBIT	CREDIT	BALANCE

NAME _____ TERMS _____

DATE	DESCRIPTION	POST. REF.	DEBIT	CREDIT	BALANCE

NAME _____ TERMS _____

DATE	DESCRIPTION	POST. REF.	DEBIT	CREDIT	BALANCE

CHAPTER 7 CHALLENGE PROBLEM (continued)

ACCOUNTS RECEIVABLE SUBSIDIARY LEDGER

NAME _____   TERMS _____

	DATE	DESCRIPTION	POST. REF.	DEBIT	CREDIT	BALANCE

Balance of Accounts Receivable account: _____

Analyze: _____

_____

CHAPTER 7 CRITICAL THINKING PROBLEM

1. _____
   _____
   _____
   _____
   _____

2. _____
   _____
   _____
   _____
   _____
   _____
   _____

3. _____
   _____
   _____
   _____
   _____
   _____

4. _____
   _____
   _____
   _____
   _____
   _____
   _____

Chapter 7 Practice Test Answer Key

Part A True-False		Part B Matching	Part C Exercises
1. F	11. F	1. f	
2. T	12. T	2. d	
3. T	13. T	3. b	
4. T	14. T	4. a	
5. F	15. T	5. e	
6. T	16. T	6. c	
7. F	17. T	7. g	
8. F	18. F		
9. T	19. F		
10. T	20. T		

Part C Exercises

1. The balance was carried over from December 2006.
2. By referring to a copy of Sales Slip 101.
3. It was most likely a sales return or allowance. Refer to the January 17 entry on page 1 of the general journal.

CHAPTER 8

Accounting for Purchases and Accounts Payable

STUDY GUIDE

Understanding the Chapter

Objectives

1. Record purchases of merchandise on credit in a three-column purchases journal. **2.** Post from the three-column purchases journal to the general ledger accounts. **3.** Post credit purchases from the purchases journal to the accounts payable subsidiary ledger. **4.** Record purchases returns and allowances in the general journal and post them to the accounts payable subsidiary ledger. **5.** Prepare a schedule of accounts payable. **6.** Compute the net delivered cost of purchases. **7.** Demonstrate a knowledge of the procedures for effective internal control of purchases. **8.** Define the accounting terms new to this chapter.

Reading Assignment

Read Chapter 8 in the textbook. Complete the textbook Section Self Review as you finish reading each section of the chapter, and the Comprehensive Self Review at the end of the chapter. Refer to the Chapter 8 Glossary or to the Glossary at the end of the book to find definitions for terms that are not familiar to you.

Activities

❏ **Thinking Critically**
Answer the *Thinking Critically* questions for Pier 1 Imports, Accounting on the Job, and Managerial Implications.

❏ **Internet Applications**
Complete the activity for Accounting on the Job.

❏ **Discussion Questions**
Answer each assigned discussion question in Chapter 8.

❏ **Exercises**
Complete each assigned exercise in Chapter 8. Use the forms provided in this SGWP. The objectives covered by an exercise are given after the exercise number. If you need help with an exercise, review the portion of the chapter related to the objective(s) covered.

❏ **Problems A/B**
Complete each assigned problem in Chapter 8. Use the forms provided in this SGWP. The objectives covered by a problem are given after the problem number. If you need help with a problem, review the portion of the chapter related to the objective(s) covered.

❏ **Challenge Problem**
Complete the challenge problem as assigned. Use the forms provided in this SGWP.

❏ **Critical Thinking Problem**
Complete the critical thinking problem as assigned. Use the forms provided in this SGWP.

❏ **Business Connections**
Complete the Business Connections activities as assigned to gain a deeper understanding of Chapter 8 concepts.

Practice Tests

Complete the Practice Tests, which cover the main points in your reading assignment. Compare your answers with those in the Practice Test Answer Key for Chapter 8 at the end of this chapter. If you have answered any questions incorrectly, review the related section of the text.

Part A True-False

For each of the following statements, circle T in the answer column if the statement is true or F if the statement is false.

T F 1. A receiving report is prepared to show the quantity of goods received and their condition.

T F 2. The special purchases journal is used to record all transactions in which merchandise or equipment is purchased on credit.

T F 3. When properly designed, a purchases journal makes posting to the general ledger unnecessary.

T F 4. The provision in the purchases journal of special columns for the invoice number, the invoice date, and the credit terms is intended to ensure payment of the bill when it is due.

T F 5. An account called **Purchases** is charged with the cost of the merchandise as it is sold.

T F 6. One of the basic advantages of the purchases journal is that the posting to **Accounts Receivable** is simplified.

T F 7. Each purchase of merchandise on credit should be recorded in the purchases journal as it occurs during the month.

T F 8. The balance of each creditor's account in the accounts payable ledger is not computed until the end of the accounting period.

T F 9. At the end of the month, the total of the Accounts Payable column in the purchases journal is debited to the **Accounts Payable** control account.

T F 10. Payments made to creditors are recorded in the cash payments journal.

T F 11. At the end of the month, the total of the payments made to creditors is debited to the **Purchases** account.

T F 12. The use of the balance ledger form makes each creditor's balance readily available.

T F 13. Within the accounts payable ledger, the accounts for creditors are arranged alphabetically or by account number.

T F 14. After all postings for a period are completed, the total of the individual balances in the accounts payable ledger should be equal to the balance of the **Accounts Payable** control account in the general ledger.

T F 15. As soon as it is recorded in the **Purchases** journal, the amount of a purchase is posted as a credit to the supplier's account in the accounts payable ledger.

T F 16. A payment is first recorded in the cash payments journal and then debited immediately to the supplier's account in the accounts payable ledger.

T F 17. The procedure for posting totals from the purchases journal remains the same, whether or not an accounts payable ledger is used.

T F 18. Freight In becomes part of the cost of purchases shown in the Cost of Goods Sold section of the income statement.

Part B Exercise   *Answer each of the following in the space provided. Make your answers complete but as brief as possible.*

A firm uses a multicolumn purchases journal with the following money columns: Accounts Payable Credit, Purchases Debit, and Freight In Debit

1. Where is the **Freight In** account shown on the income statement?

   _____

   _____

   _____

   _____

2. The figures of which column are used to update the accounts payable ledger?

   _____

   _____

   _____

   _____

3. Where would you record the purchase of office equipment on open account credit terms?

   _____

   _____

   _____

   _____

4. If the buyer pays freight charges directly to the carrier on a purchase of merchandise, where is the freight transaction recorded?

   _____

   _____

   _____

   _____

5. How is the accuracy of the totals verified at the end of the month?

   _____

   _____

   _____

   _____

6. Which columns are totaled and summary posted to the general ledger?

   _____

   _____

   _____

   _____

7. How is the **Purchases** account classified?

   _____

   _____

   _____

   _____

Demonstration Problem

Frontier Office Supply is a retail business that sells office equipment, furniture, and office supplies. Its credit purchases and purchases returns and allowances for the month of October 2007 follow. The general ledger accounts used to record these transactions are given below.

Instructions

1. Open the general ledger accounts and enter the balance of Accounts Payable for October 1, 2007.

2. Using the list of creditors that follows, open the accounts in the accounts payable subsidiary ledger and enter the account balances for October 1, 2007.

3. Record the transactions in a purchases journal, page 12, and a general journal, page 30.

4. Post individual entries from the purchases journal to the accounts payable subsidiary ledger, then post from the general journal to the general ledger and accounts payable subsidiary ledger.

5. Total, prove, and rule the purchases journal as of October 31, 2007.

6. Post the column totals from the purchases journal to the appropriate general ledger accounts.

7. Compute the net delivered cost of the firm's purchases for the month.

8. Prepare a schedule of accounts payable for October 31, 2007.

9. Check the total of the schedule of accounts payable against the balance of the **Accounts Payable** account in the general ledger. The two amounts should be equal.

GENERAL LEDGER ACCOUNTS

205 Accounts Payable	$18,900 Cr.
501 Purchases	
502 Freight In	
503 Purchases Returns and Allowances	

CREDITORS

Name	Terms	Balance
Essential Office Supplies	n/30	
Dallas Office Supply	n/60	$2,320
Davis Office Products	n/30	
Metroplex Office Center	2/10, n/30	5,670
Thomas Copy and Paper	1/10, n/30	10,910

DATE	TRANSACTIONS
October 4	Purchased desks for $9,160 plus a freight charge of $280 from Davis Office Products, Invoice 3124 dated September 30, terms payable in 30 days.
9	Purchased computers for $6,550 from Essential Office Supplies, Invoice 7129 dated October 4, net due and payable in 30 days.
11	Received Credit Memo 165 for $600 from Davis Office Products as an allowance for slightly damaged but usable desks purchased on Invoice 3124 of September 30.
16	Purchased file cabinets for $2,720 plus a freight charge of $124 from Dallas Office Supply, Invoice 9088 dated October 11, terms of 60 days.
21	Purchased electronic calculators for $2,200 from Essential Office Supplies, Invoice 2765 dated October 16, net due and payable in 30 days.
24	Purchased laser printer paper for $3,350 plus a freight charge of $320 from Thomas Copy and Paper on Invoice 4891 dated October 19, terms of 1/10, n/30.
29	Received Credit Memo 629 for $440 from Essential Office Supplies for defective calculators that were returned. The calculators were originally purchased on Invoice 2765 of October 16.
31	Purchased office chairs for $3,900 plus a freight charge of $136 from Metroplex Office Center, Invoice 966 dated October 26, terms of 2/10, n/30.

SOLUTION

PURCHASES JOURNAL

DATE		CUSTOMER'S NAME	INVOICE NUMBER	INVOICE DATE	TERMS	POST. REF.	ACCOUNTS PAYABLE CREDIT	PURCHASES DEBIT	FREIGHT IN DEBIT
2007									
Oct.	4	Davis Office Products	3124	9/30	n/30		9 4 4 0 00	9 1 6 0 00	2 8 0 00
	9	Essential Office Supplies	7129	10/4	n/30		6 5 5 0 00	6 5 5 0 00	
	16	Dallas Office Supply	9088	10/11	n/60		2 8 4 4 00	2 7 2 0 00	1 2 4 00
	21	Essential Office Supplies	2765	10/16	n/30		2 2 0 0 00	2 2 0 0 00	
	24	Thomas Copy & Paper							
		Company	4891	10/19	1/10, n/30		3 6 7 0 00	3 3 5 0 00	3 2 0 00
	31	Metroplex Office Center	966	10/26	2/10, n/30		4 0 3 6 00	3 9 0 0 00	1 3 6 00
	31						28 7 4 0 00	27 8 8 0 00	8 6 0 00

GENERAL JOURNAL

	DATE		DESCRIPTION	POST. REF.	DEBIT	CREDIT	
1	2007						1
2	Oct.	11	Accounts Payable/Davis Office Products	205 ✔	6 0 0 00		2
3			Purchases Returns and Allowances	503		6 0 0 00	3
4			Received Credit Memo 165 for				4
5			damaged merchandise; original				5
6			purchase was made on Invoice 3124,				6
7			September 30, 2007				7
8							8
9		29	Accounts Payable/Essential Office Supplies	205 ✔	4 4 0 00		9
10			Purchases Returns & Allowances	503		4 4 0 00	10
11			Received Credit Memo 629 for damaged				11
12			merchandise that was returned;				12
13			original purchase was made on				13
14			Invoice 2765, October 16.				14
15							15

SOLUTION (continued)

GENERAL LEDGER

ACCOUNT __Accounts Payable__   ACCOUNT NO. ____205__

DATE		DESCRIPTION	POST. REF.	DEBIT	CREDIT	BALANCE DEBIT	BALANCE CREDIT
2007							
Oct.	1	Balance	✔				18 9 0 0 00
	11		J30	6 0 0 00			18 3 0 0 00
	29		J30	4 4 0 00			17 8 6 0 00
	31		P12		28 7 4 0 00		46 6 0 0 00

ACCOUNT __Purchases__   ACCOUNT NO. ____501__

DATE		DESCRIPTION	POST. REF.	DEBIT	CREDIT	BALANCE DEBIT	BALANCE CREDIT
2007							
Oct.	31		P12	27 8 8 0 00		27 8 8 0 00	

ACCOUNT __Freight In__   ACCOUNT NO. ____502__

DATE		DESCRIPTION	POST. REF.	DEBIT	CREDIT	BALANCE DEBIT	BALANCE CREDIT
2007							
Oct.	31		P12	8 6 0 00		8 6 0 00	

ACCOUNT __Purchases Returns and Allowances__   ACCOUNT NO. ____503__

DATE		DESCRIPTION	POST. REF.	DEBIT	CREDIT	BALANCE DEBIT	BALANCE CREDIT
2007							
Oct.	11		J30		6 0 0 00		6 0 0 00
	29		J30		4 4 0 00		1 0 4 0 00

Purchases	$27,880
Freight In	860
Delivered Cost of Purchases	$28,740
Less Purchases Returns and Allowances	1,040
Net Delivered Cost of Purchases	$27,700

STUDY GUIDE

SOLUTION (continued)

ACCOUNTS PAYABLE SUBSIDIARY LEDGER

NAME **Essential Office Supplies** TERMS **n/30**

DATE		DESCRIPTION	POST. REF.	DEBIT	CREDIT	BALANCE
2007						
Oct.	9	Invoice 7129, 10/4/07	P12		6 5 5 0 00	6 5 5 0 00
	21	Invoice 2765, 10/16/07	P12		2 2 0 0 00	8 7 5 0 00
	29	CM 629	J30	4 4 0 00		8 3 1 0 00

NAME **Dallas Office Supply** TERMS **n/60**

DATE		DESCRIPTION	POST. REF.	DEBIT	CREDIT	BALANCE
2007						
Oct.	1	Balance	✔			2 3 2 0 00
	16	Invoice 9088, 10/11/07	P12		2 8 4 4 00	5 1 6 4 00

NAME **Davis Office Products** TERMS **n/30**

DATE		DESCRIPTION	POST. REF.	DEBIT	CREDIT	BALANCE
2007						
Oct.	4	Invoice 3124, 9/30/07	P12		9 4 4 0 00	9 4 4 0 00
	11	CM 165	J30	6 0 0 00		8 8 4 0 00

NAME **Metroplex Office Center** TERMS **2/10, n/30**

DATE		DESCRIPTION	POST. REF.	DEBIT	CREDIT	BALANCE
20-07						
Oct.	1	Balance	✔			5 6 7 0 00
	31	Invoice 966, 10/26/07	P12		4 0 3 6 00	9 7 0 6 00

NAME **Thomas Copy and Paper Company** TERMS **1/10, n/30**

DATE		DESCRIPTION	POST. REF.	DEBIT	CREDIT	BALANCE
2007						
Oct.	1	Balance	✔			10 9 1 0 00
	24	Invoice 4891, 10/19/07	P12		3 6 7 0 00	14 5 8 0 00

SOLUTION (continued)

Frontier Office Supply

Schedule of Accounts Payable

October 31, 2007

Essential Office Supplies	8 3 1 0	00
Dallas Office Supply	5 1 6 4	00
Davis Office Products	8 8 4 0	00
Metroplex Office Center	9 7 0 6	00
Thomas Copy and Paper Company	14 5 8 0	00
Total	46 6 0 0	00

WORKING PAPERS

Name _____

EXERCISE 8.1

1. _____   4. _____

2. _____   5. _____

3. _____   6. _____

EXERCISE 8.2

	Dr.	Cr.		Dr.	Cr.
1.	_____	_____	4.	_____	_____
2.	_____	_____	5.	_____	_____
3.	_____	_____	6.	_____	_____

EXERCISE 8.3

PURCHASES JOURNAL   PAGE _____

DATE	PURCHASED FROM	INVOICE NUMBER	INVOICE DATE	TERMS	POST. REF.	ACCOUNTS PAYABLE CREDIT	PURCHASES DEBIT	FREIGHT IN DEBIT

EXERCISE 8.4

GENERAL JOURNAL   PAGE _____

	DATE	DESCRIPTION	POST. REF.	DEBIT	CREDIT	
1						1
2						2
3						3
4						4
5						5
6						6
7						7
8						8
9						9
10						10

EXERCISE 8.5

GENERAL JOURNAL   PAGE _____

	DATE	DESCRIPTION	POST. REF.	DEBIT	CREDIT	
1						1
2						2
3						3
4						4
5						5
6						6
7						7

EXERCISE 8.6

_____

_____

_____

_____

_____

EXERCISE 8.7

a. _____

_____

b. _____

_____

c. _____

d. _____

_____

EXERCISE 8.8

a. _____

b. _____

c. _____

d. _____

PROBLEM 8.1A or 8.1B

PURCHASES JOURNAL

PAGE _____

DATE	PURCHASED FROM	INVOICE NUMBER	INVOICE DATE	TERMS	POST. REF.	ACCOUNTS PAYABLE CREDIT	PURCHASES DEBIT	FREIGHT IN DEBIT
June 1	Jones Company	4241	May 27	60 day		2175	1995	180
8	Camera and Films	1102	June 4	45 day		1390	1390	
12	Optical Supply	728	June 9	1/10		906	906	
20	Camera and Films	1146	June 15	45 day		1125	1050	75
23	Chicago Case Comp	308	June 18	45 d		1990	1990	
29	Zant Corp	5037	June 25	2/10		2540	2470	120
						10126	9805	375

GENERAL JOURNAL

PAGE _____

	DATE	DESCRIPTION	POST. REF.	DEBIT	CREDIT	
1	June 16	A/P	501	375		1
2		Purchases Return and Allowan	503		375	2
3						3
4						4
5						5
6	June 30	A/P		240		6
7		Purchases R/A			240	7
8						8
9						9
10						10
11						11
12						12
13						13
14						14
15						15
16						16
17						17
18						18
19						19

PROBLEM 8.1A or 8.1B (continued)

GENERAL LEDGER

ACCOUNT __Accounts Payable__   ACCOUNT NO. __205__

DATE	DESCRIPTION	POST. REF.	DEBIT	CREDIT	BALANCE DEBIT	BALANCE CREDIT
				6126		10126
			375			4751
			240			4511

ACCOUNT __Purchases__   ACCOUNT NO. __501__

DATE	DESCRIPTION	POST. REF.	DEBIT	CREDIT	BALANCE DEBIT	BALANCE CREDIT
	Balance		8005		8005	

ACCOUNT __Frieght IN__   ACCOUNT NO. __502__

DATE	DESCRIPTION	POST. REF.	DEBIT	CREDIT	BALANCE DEBIT	BALANCE CREDIT
	Balance		375		375	

ACCOUNT __Purchases Returns and Allowances__   ACCOUNT NO. __503__

DATE	DESCRIPTION	POST. REF.	DEBIT	CREDIT	BALANCE DEBIT	BALANCE CREDIT
				375		
				240		615

Purchases   8005
Frieght In   375
A/P   10,126
Purchases R/A 615

Analyze: _____

PROBLEM 8.2A or 8.2B

ACCOUNTS PAYABLE SUBSIDIARY LEDGER

NAME _____ TERMS _____

	DATE	DESCRIPTION	POST. REF.	DEBIT	CREDIT	BALANCE

NAME _____ TERMS _____

	DATE	DESCRIPTION	POST. REF.	DEBIT	CREDIT	BALANCE

NAME _____ TERMS _____

	DATE	DESCRIPTION	POST. REF.	DEBIT	CREDIT	BALANCE

NAME _____ TERMS _____

	DATE	DESCRIPTION	POST. REF.	DEBIT	CREDIT	BALANCE

NAME _____ TERMS _____

	DATE	DESCRIPTION	POST. REF.	DEBIT	CREDIT	BALANCE

PROBLEM 8.2A or 8.2B (continued)

Analyze:

EXTRA FORM

PROBLEM 8.3A or 8.3B

PURCHASES JOURNAL   PAGE _____

DATE	PURCHASED FROM	INVOICE NUMBER	INVOICE DATE	TERMS	POST. REF.	ACCOUNTS PAYABLE CREDIT	PURCHASES DEBIT	FREIGHT IN DEBIT

GENERAL JOURNAL   PAGE _____

	DATE	DESCRIPTION	POST. REF.	DEBIT	CREDIT	
1						1
2						2
3						3
4						4
5						5
6						6
7						7
8						8
9						9
10						10
11						11
12						12
13						13
14						14
15						15

PROBLEM 8.3A or 8.3B (continued)

GENERAL LEDGER

ACCOUNT _____ ACCOUNT NO. _____

DATE	DESCRIPTION	POST. REF.	DEBIT	CREDIT	BALANCE	
					DEBIT	CREDIT

ACCOUNT _____ ACCOUNT NO. _____

DATE	DESCRIPTION	POST. REF.	DEBIT	CREDIT	BALANCE	
					DEBIT	CREDIT

ACCOUNT _____ ACCOUNT NO. _____

DATE	DESCRIPTION	POST. REF.	DEBIT	CREDIT	BALANCE	
					DEBIT	CREDIT

ACCOUNT _____ ACCOUNT NO. _____

DATE	DESCRIPTION	POST. REF.	DEBIT	CREDIT	BALANCE	
					DEBIT	CREDIT

_____

_____

_____

_____

_____

_____

PROBLEM 8.3A or 8.3B (continued)

ACCOUNTS PAYABLE SUBSIDIARY LEDGER

NAME _____ TERMS _____

	DATE	DESCRIPTION	POST. REF.	DEBIT	CREDIT	BALANCE

NAME _____ TERMS _____

	DATE	DESCRIPTION	POST. REF.	DEBIT	CREDIT	BALANCE

NAME _____ TERMS _____

	DATE	DESCRIPTION	POST. REF.	DEBIT	CREDIT	BALANCE

NAME _____ TERMS _____

	DATE	DESCRIPTION	POST. REF.	DEBIT	CREDIT	BALANCE

NAME _____ TERMS _____

	DATE	DESCRIPTION	POST. REF.	DEBIT	CREDIT	BALANCE

PROBLEM 8.3A or 8.3B (continued)

Analyze: _____

EXTRA FORMS

NAME_____ TERMS _____

	DATE	DESCRIPTION	POST. REF.	DEBIT	CREDIT	BALANCE

NAME_____ TERMS _____

	DATE	DESCRIPTION	POST. REF.	DEBIT	CREDIT	BALANCE

PROBLEM 8.4A or 8.4B

PURCHASES JOURNAL

PAGE _____

DATE	PURCHASED FROM	INVOICE NUMBER	INVOICE DATE	TERMS	POST. REF.	ACCOUNTS PAYABLE CREDIT	PURCHASES DEBIT	FREIGHT IN DEBIT
Sep 3	Dalton Office Furn	4513	Aug 29	30day		8130	7920	212

GENERAL JOURNAL

PAGE _____

	DATE	DESCRIPTION	POST. REF.	DEBIT	CREDIT	
1						1
2						2
3						3
4						4
5						5
6						6
7						7
8						8
9						9
10						10
11						11
12						12
13						13
14						14
15						15

PROBLEM 8.4A or 8.4B (continued)

GENERAL LEDGER

ACCOUNT _____ ACCOUNT NO. _____

DATE		DESCRIPTION	POST. REF.	DEBIT	CREDIT	BALANCE	
						DEBIT	CREDIT
							29256

ACCOUNT _____ ACCOUNT NO. _____

DATE		DESCRIPTION	POST. REF.	DEBIT	CREDIT	BALANCE	
						DEBIT	CREDIT

ACCOUNT _____ ACCOUNT NO. _____

DATE		DESCRIPTION	POST. REF.	DEBIT	CREDIT	BALANCE	
						DEBIT	CREDIT

ACCOUNT _____ ACCOUNT NO. _____

DATE		DESCRIPTION	POST. REF.	DEBIT	CREDIT	BALANCE	
						DEBIT	CREDIT

Net Delivered Cost of Purchases

_____

_____

_____

_____

_____

_____

PROBLEM 8.4A or 8.4B (continued)

ACCOUNTS PAYABLE SUBSIDIARY LEDGER

NAME _____ TERMS _____

DATE	DESCRIPTION	POST. REF.	DEBIT	CREDIT	BALANCE

NAME _____ TERMS _____

DATE	DESCRIPTION	POST. REF.	DEBIT	CREDIT	BALANCE

NAME _____ TERMS _____

DATE	DESCRIPTION	POST. REF.	DEBIT	CREDIT	BALANCE

NAME _____ TERMS _____

DATE	DESCRIPTION	POST. REF.	DEBIT	CREDIT	BALANCE

NAME _____ TERMS _____

DATE	DESCRIPTION	POST. REF.	DEBIT	CREDIT	BALANCE

PROBLEM 8.4A or 8.4B (continued)

Analyze:

EXTRA FORM

CHAPTER 8 CHALLENGE PROBLEM

PURCHASES JOURNAL

PAGE _____

DATE	PURCHASED FROM	INVOICE NUMBER	INVOICE DATE	TERMS	POST. REF.	ACCOUNTS PAYABLE CREDIT	PURCHASES DEBIT	FREIGHT IN DEBIT
Jan 3	Fashion Center	101	Dec 26	30d		5112	5000	112
Jan 5	Hand Bag depot	223	Dec 28	2/10 n		3509	3420	89
7	House of Styles	556	Jan 3	2/10 n30		3969	3900	69
9	M.W.P.S. Company	110	Jan 5	n 30		2360	2360	
12	International Eye	104	Jan 9	2/10 n30		5529	5400	129
18	Mr John Shoes	118	Jan 17	n 60		3200	3120	80
25	Hosiery Warehouse	1012	Jan 20	2/10 n30		900	400	
29	M.W.P.S. Company	315	Jan 26	N/30		1600	1600	
31	S.O.W.D shop	1044	Jan 27	2/10 n/30		5475	5250	225
						31704	31010	703

SALES JOURNAL

PAGE _____

	DATE	SALES SLIP NO.	CUSTOMER'S NAME	POST. REF.	ACCOUNTS RECEIVABLE DEBIT	SALES TAX PAYABLE CREDIT	SALES CREDIT	
1	Jan 4	101	Sarah Valdez		864	64	800	1
2	5	102	Linda Canton		432	32	400	2
3	6	103	Teresa Collins		432	32	400	3
4	10	104	Demetria Davis		648	48	600	4
5	14	105	Jeraldine Wells		540	40	500	5
6	17	106	Amalia Rodriguez		864	64	800	6
7	21	107	Rosabla Vasquez		2160	160	2000	7
8	24	108	Shernye Samuels		432	32	400	8
9	25	109	Cecila Lin		324	24	300	9
10	29	100	Tonya Ennis		648	48	600	10
11	31	111	Isabel James		810	60	750	11
12					8154	604	7550	12
13								13
14								14
15								15

CHAPTER 8 CHALLENGE PROBLEM (continued)

ACCOUNTS PAYABLE SUBSIDIARY LEDGER

NAME _____Fashion Center_____ TERMS _____

DATE	DESCRIPTION	POST. REF.	DEBIT	CREDIT	BALANCE
Jun 3	Balance			5112	5112

NAME _____Handbag Depot_____ TERMS _____

DATE	DESCRIPTION	POST. REF.	DEBIT	CREDIT	BALANCE
June 5	Balance			3560	3560

NAME _____House of Styles_____ TERMS _____

DATE	DESCRIPTION	POST. REF.	DEBIT	CREDIT	BALANCE
Jun 7	Balance			3968	3968

NAME _____Modern Women Pants and Suits_____ TERMS _____

DATE	DESCRIPTION	POST. REF.	DEBIT	CREDIT	BALANCE
Jun 9				2360	2360
Jun 29	Balance			1600	3960

NAME _____International Executive_____ TERMS _____

DATE	DESCRIPTION	POST. REF.	DEBIT	CREDIT	BALANCE
Jun 12	Balance			5524	5524

NAME _____Mr. John's Shoes_____ TERMS _____

DATE	DESCRIPTION	POST. REF.	DEBIT	CREDIT	BALANCE
June 19	Balance			3200	3200

CHAPTER 8 CHALLENGE PROBLEM (continued)

ACCOUNTS PAYABLE SUBSIDIARY LEDGER

NAME ____Hosiery Warehouse____ TERMS _____

DATE	DESCRIPTION	POST. REF.	DEBIT	CREDIT	BALANCE
Jun 5	Balance			900	900

NAME ____Special Occasion Wholesale Dress Shop____ TERMS _____

DATE	DESCRIPTION	POST. REF.	DEBIT	CREDIT	BALANCE
J 31	Balance			5475	5475

ACCOUNTS RECEIVABLE SUBSIDIARY LEDGER

NAME ____Sarah Valdez____ TERMS _____

DATE	DESCRIPTION	POST. REF.	DEBIT	CREDIT	BALANCE
	A/R		864		864

NAME ____Linda Carter____ TERMS _____

DATE	DESCRIPTION	POST. REF.	DEBIT	CREDIT	BALANCE
	A/R		432		432

NAME ____Teresa Collins____ TERMS _____

DATE	DESCRIPTION	POST. REF.	DEBIT	CREDIT	BALANCE
	A/R		432		434

CHAPTER 8 CHALLENGE PROBLEM (continued)

ACCOUNTS RECEIVABLE SUBSIDIARY LEDGER

NAME _____Demetria Davis_____ TERMS _____

DATE		DESCRIPTION	POST. REF.	DEBIT	CREDIT	BALANCE
		A/R		648		648

NAME _____Jeraldine Wells_____ TERMS _____

DATE		DESCRIPTION	POST. REF.	DEBIT	CREDIT	BALANCE
		A/R		540		540

NAME _____Amalia Rodriguez_____ TERMS _____

DATE		DESCRIPTION	POST. REF.	DEBIT	CREDIT	BALANCE
		A/R		864		864

NAME _____Rosabla Vasquez_____ TERMS _____

DATE		DESCRIPTION	POST. REF.	DEBIT	CREDIT	BALANCE
		A/R		2160		2160

NAME _____Sherrte Samuels_____ TERMS _____

DATE		DESCRIPTION	POST. REF.	DEBIT	CREDIT	BALANCE
		A/R		432		432

NAME _____Cecila Lin_____ TERMS _____

DATE		DESCRIPTION	POST. REF.	DEBIT	CREDIT	BALANCE
		A/R		324		324

CHAPTER 8 CHALLENGE PROBLEM (continued)

ACCOUNTS RECEIVABLE SUBSIDIARY LEDGER

NAME __Tonya Ennis__ TERMS _____

	DATE	DESCRIPTION	POST. REF.	DEBIT	CREDIT	BALANCE
		A/R		648		648

NAME __Isabel James__ TERMS _____

	DATE	DESCRIPTION	POST. REF.	DEBIT	CREDIT	BALANCE
		A/R		810		810

GENERAL LEDGER

ACCOUNT __Accounts Payable__ ACCOUNT NO. _____

	DATE	DESCRIPTION	POST. REF.	DEBIT	CREDIT	BALANCE DEBIT	BALANCE CREDIT
		Balance			31713		31704

ACCOUNT __Purchases__ ACCOUNT NO. _____

	DATE	DESCRIPTION	POST. REF.	DEBIT	CREDIT	BALANCE DEBIT	BALANCE CREDIT
		Balance		31010			31010

ACCOUNT __Freight In__ ACCOUNT NO. _____

	DATE	DESCRIPTION	POST. REF.	DEBIT	CREDIT	BALANCE DEBIT	BALANCE CREDIT
		Balance		703		703	

ACCOUNT __A/R__ ACCOUNT NO. _____

	DATE	DESCRIPTION	POST. REF.	DEBIT	CREDIT	BALANCE DEBIT	BALANCE CREDIT
		Balance		8154			8154

GENERAL LEDGER

ACCOUNT _____Sales Tax Payable_____   ACCOUNT NO. _____

DATE	DESCRIPTION	POST. REF.	DEBIT	CREDIT	BALANCE DEBIT	BALANCE CREDIT
	Balance			604		604

ACCOUNT _____Sales_____   ACCOUNT NO. _____

DATE	DESCRIPTION	POST. REF.	DEBIT	CREDIT	BALANCE DEBIT	BALANCE CREDIT
	Balance			7950		7950

_____Schedule of Accounts Payable_____

Fashion Center	5112
Handbag Depot	3560
House of Styles	3968
Modern Women Pants Suits Company	3960
International Executive	5529
Mr Johns Shoes	3200
Hosiery Warehouse	900
Special Occasional Whole Sale Dress Shop	5475
	31704

CHAPTER 8 CHALLENGE PROBLEM (continued)

Schedule of Accounts Receivable

Sarah Valdez	864
Linda Carter	432
Teresa Collins	432
Demetria Davis	648
Jeraldine Wells	540
Amalia Rodriguez	864
Rosabla Vasquez	2160
Sherrye Samuels	432
Cecila Lin	324
Tonya Ennis	648
Isabel James	810
	8154

Analyze: _____
_____
_____
_____
_____
_____
_____

CHAPTER 8 CRITICAL THINKING PROBLEM

_____

_____

_____

_____

_____

_____

_____

_____

_____

_____

_____

_____

_____

_____

_____

_____

_____

_____

_____

_____

_____

_____

_____

_____

_____

_____

Chapter 8 Practice Test Answer Key

Part A True-False

1. T	10. T
2. F	11. F
3. F	12. T
4. T	13. T
5. F	14. T
6. F	15. T
7. T	16. T
8. F	17. T
9. F	18. T

Part B Exercises

1. In the Cost of Goods Sold Section.
2. The Accounts Payable Column.
3. The General Journal.
4. It is not recorded in the purchases journal at all; it is entered in the cash payments journal.
5. Accounts Payable Credit = Purchases Debit + Freight In Debit.
6. All Columns.
7. An Expense.

CHAPTER 9

Cash Receipts, Cash Payments, and Banking Procedures

STUDY GUIDE

Understanding the Chapter

Objectives	**1.** Record cash receipts in a cash receipts journal. **2.** Account for cash short or over. **3.** Post from the cash receipts journal to subsidiary and general ledgers. **4.** Record cash payments in a cash payments journal. **5.** Post from the cash payments journal to subsidiary and general ledgers. **6.** Demonstrate a knowledge of procedures for a petty cash fund. **7.** Demonstrate a knowledge of internal control routines for cash. **8.** Write a check, endorse checks, prepare a bank deposit slip, and maintain a checkbook balance. **9.** Reconcile the monthly bank statement. **10.** Record any adjusting entries required from the bank reconciliation. **11.** Define accounting terms new to this chapter.
Reading Assignment	Read Chapter 9 in the textbook. Complete the Section Self Review as you finish reading each section of the chapter, and the Comprehensive Self Review at the end of the chapter. Refer to the Chapter 9 Glossary or to the Glossary at the end of the book to find definitions for terms that are not familiar to you.

Activities

❏ **Thinking Critically**	Answer the *Thinking Critically* questions for H&R Block, Computers in Accounting, and Managerial Implications
❏ **Internet Application**	Complete the activity for Computers in Accounting.
❏ **Discussion Questions**	Answer each assigned review question in Chapter 9.
❏ **Exercises**	Complete each assigned exercise in Chapter 9. Use the forms provided in this SGWP. The objectives covered by an exercise are given after the exercise number. If you need help with an exercise, review the portion of the chapter related to the objective(s) covered.
❏ **Problems A/B**	Complete each assigned problem in Chapter 9. Use the forms provided in this SGWP. The objectives covered by a problem are given after the problem number. If you need help with a problem review the portion of the chapter related to the objective(s) covered.
❏ **Challenge Problem**	Complete the challenge problem as assigned. Use the forms provided in this SGWP.
❏ **Critical Thinking Problem**	Complete the critical thinking problem as assigned. Use the forms provided in this SGWP.
❏ **Business Connections**	Complete the Business Connections activities as assigned to gain a deeper understanding of Chapter 9 concepts.

Practice Tests

Complete the Practice Tests, which cover the main points in your reading assignment. Compare your answers with those in the Practice Test Answer Key for Chapter 9 at the end of this chapter. If you have answered any questions incorrectly, review the related section of the text.

Part A True-False *For each of the following statements, circle T in the answer column if the statement is true or F if the statement is false.*

T F **1.** The abbreviation "CP5" in the Posting Reference column of a ledger account indicates that the posting was made from the cash payments journal on the fifth day of the month.

T F **2.** When posting from the cash payments journal at the end of the month, the accountant posts the total cash payments as a single credit to cash.

T F **3.** The check to replenish the petty cash fund is written for an amount sufficient to restore the fund to its established balance.

T F **4.** The petty cash analysis sheet is a memorandum record of petty cash payments rather than a record of original entry.

T F **5.** Each petty cash payment is entered separately in the cash payments journal.

T F **6.** An adequate system of internal control over cash will provide for safeguarding both incoming and outgoing funds.

T F **7.** Correct internal control procedures require that the approval for paying all bills, writing all checks, and signing all checks should be the responsibility of the same person.

T F **8.** Except for petty cash payments, all payments should be made by check.

T F **9.** Internal controls are not necessary if payments are made by check.

T F **10.** The best form of endorsement for business purposes is the restrictive endorsement, which limits the use of the check to a stated purpose.

T F **11.** The money represented by deposited checks becomes available for use as soon as the deposit is made.

T F **12.** Checks made payable to cash or to bearer need not be endorsed when deposited.

T F **13.** Checks can be identified on a deposit slip by the use of the American Bankers Association transit numbers.

T F **14.** Only checks are listed on the deposit slip.

T F **15.** Cash received by mail should be deposited by a person other than the one who accepts and lists it.

T F **16. Cash Short or Over** is a general ledger account that normally has a debit balance because cash tends to be short more often than over.

T F **17.** The **Sales Tax Payable** account represents an expense of the business.

T F **18.** The title of a special journal makes it possible to omit much of the explanation that would be needed in a general journal entry.

T F **19.** A cash investment by the owner in a business should not be recorded in the cash receipts journal.

T F **20.** Account numbers are recorded below the totals of each column as each summary posting from the cash payments journal is completed.

T F **21.** The Other Accounts Debit column of a cash payments journal is used to record the debits that are to be posted individually.

Part B Matching *For each numbered item, choose the matching term from the box and write the identifying letter in the answer column.*

_____ 1. The process by which a single amount is posted instead of each entry being posted separately.

_____ 2. A written promise to pay a specific amount at a specific time.

_____ 3. A system designed to safeguard assets and to help ensure the accuracy and reliability of accounting records.

_____ 4. A form received from the bank showing all transactions recorded in the depositor's account during the month.

_____ 5. Receipts that have been deposited and entered in the firm's accounting records but have not yet been entered on the bank's records.

_____ 6. A form on which all cash and cash items are listed before they are placed in the bank.

_____ 7. Checks issued and recorded that have not been paid by the bank.

_____ 8. A check on which payment has been refused because of too few funds in the issuer's account.

_____ 9. The person or firm from whose account a check is to be paid.

_____ 10. The form that contains all the information necessary for journalizing a transaction paid by check.

_____ 11. The firm or person designated on the check to receive payment.

_____ 12. The process of determining why a difference exists between the firm's accounting records and the bank records and bringing them into balance.

a. NSF Check
b. Deposit in Transit
c. Outstanding checks
d. Bank reconciliation
e. Bank statement
f. Stub
g. Payee
h. Drawer
i. Deposit slip
j. Promissory note
k. Summary posting
l. Internal control

Demonstration Problem

On June 2, 2007, Seymore Realty received its May bank statement. Enclosed with the bank statement, shown below, was a debit memorandum for $140 for a NSF check issued by Calvin Reed. The firm's checkbook contained the information shown below about deposits made and checks issued during May. The balance of the **Cash** account and the checkbook on May 31 was $36,860.

Instructions

1. Prepare a bank reconciliation statement for Seymore Realty as of May 31, 2007.

2. Record general journal entries for any items on the bank reconciliation statement that must be journalized. Date the entries June 2, 2007.

May 1	Balance	$40,592
1	Check 177	400
1	Check 178	800
7	Deposit	2,600
8	Check 180	900
12	Check 181	6,000
17	Check 182	720
19	Deposit	680
22	Check 183	88
23	Check 184	592
26	Deposit	1,748
29	Check 185	60
30	Deposit	800
		$36,860

First Texas National Bank

Seymore Realty
4312 Pauline Street
Dallas, TX 75632-0989

ACCOUNT NO. 77546798
PERIOD ENDING: May 31, 2007

CHECK NO.	AMOUNT	DATE	DESCRIPTION	BALANCE
			Balance last statement	40,592.00
177	400.00	6/1		40,192.00
178	800.00	6/4		39,392.00
	2,600.00	6/7	Deposit	41,992.00
180	900.00	6/8		41,092.00
181	6,000.00	6/12		35,092.00
	140.00	6/12	Debit Memorandum	34,952.00
182	720.00	6/17		34,232.00
	680.00	6/19	Deposit	34,912.00
183	88.00	6/22		34,824.00
	1,748.00	6/26	Deposit	36,572.00
	10.00	6/29	Service Charge	36,562.00

SOLUTION

Seymore Realty

Bank Reconciliation Statement

May 31, 2007

Balance on Bank Statement				36 5 6 2 00
Additions:				
Deposit of May 30 in Transit			8 0 0 00	
				37 3 6 2 00
Deductions for Outstanding Checks:				
Check 184 of May 23	5 9 2 00			
Check 185 of May 29	6 0 00			
Total Checks Outstanding			6 5 2 00	
Adjusted Bank Balance				36 7 1 0 00
Balance in Books				36 8 6 0 00
Deductions:				
NSF Check	1 4 0 00			
Bank Service Charge	1 0 00		1 5 0 00	
Adjusted Book Balance				36 7 1 0 00

GENERAL JOURNAL

PAGE 17

	DATE		DESCRIPTION	POST. REF.	DEBIT	CREDIT	
1	2007						1
2	June	2	Accounts Receivable/Calvin Reed		1 4 0 00		2
3			Cash			1 4 0 00	3
4			To record NSF check Returned by bank				4
5							5
6		3	Miscellaneous Expense		1 0 00		6
7			Cash			1 0 00	7
8			To record bank service charge for May				8
9							9

WORKING PAPERS

EXERCISES 9.1, 9.2

EXERCISE 9.1

CASH RECEIPTS JOURNAL

PAGE ____

DATE	DESCRIPTION	POST. REF.	ACCOUNTS RECEIVABLE CREDIT	SALES TAX PAYABLE CREDIT	SALES CREDIT	OTHER ACCOUNTS CREDIT — ACCOUNT NAME	POST. REF.	AMOUNT	CASH DEBIT
9 1			6048	498	5660	Cash Short/over		16	6164
9 2	James Floyd		700						720
9 3				420	5050				5200
						Cash		1000	1000
9 4			6912	513	6900	Cash Short/over		(30)	6382

EXERCISE 9.2

CASH PAYMENTS JOURNAL

PAGE ____

DATE	CK. NO.	DESCRIPTION	ACCOUNTS PAYABLE DEBIT	POST. REF.	OTHER ACCOUNTS DEBIT — ACCOUNT NAME	POST. REF.	AMOUNT	PURCHASES DISCOUNT CREDIT	CASH CREDIT
		Carter Company			Rent Expense		2400		2400
					Equipment		10250		10250
					S.T.P		1340		1340
		Walter Company	1500		Merchandise		1670	30	1470
									2675
		Susan Anderson			Drawing		1800		1800

EXERCISES 9.3, 9.4

EXERCISE 9.3

CASH PAYMENTS JOURNAL

PAGE _____

DATE	CK. NO.	DESCRIPTION	POST. REF.	ACCOUNTS PAYABLE DEBIT	OTHER ACCOUNTS DEBIT			PURCHASES DISCOUNT CREDIT	CASH CREDIT
					ACCOUNT NAME	POST. REF.	AMOUNT		

EXERCISE 9.4

CASH PAYMENTS JOURNAL

PAGE _____

DATE	CK. NO.	DESCRIPTION	POST. REF.	ACCOUNTS PAYABLE DEBIT	OTHER ACCOUNTS DEBIT			PURCHASES DISCOUNT CREDIT	CASH CREDIT
					ACCOUNT NAME	POST. REF.	AMOUNT		

EXERCISE 9.5

_____

_____

GENERAL JOURNAL

PAGE _____

	DATE	DESCRIPTION	POST. REF.	DEBIT	CREDIT	
1						1
2						2
3						3
4						4
5						5
6						6
7						7
8						8
9						9
10						10
11						11
12						12
13						13
14						14

EXERCISE 9.6

	Bank Balance	Book Balance	Accounting Entry
1.			
2.			
3.			
4.			
5.			
6.			
7.			

EXERCISE 9.7

_____
_____

EXERCISE 9.7 (continued)

GENERAL JOURNAL

	DATE	DESCRIPTION	POST. REF.	DEBIT	CREDIT	
1						1
2						2
3						3
4						4
5						5
6						6
7						7
8						8
9						9
10						10
11						11

PROBLEM 9.1A or 9.1B

CASH RECEIPTS JOURNAL

DATE	DESCRIPTION	POST. REF.	ACCOUNTS RECEIVABLE CREDIT	SALES TAX PAYABLE CREDIT	SALES CREDIT	OTHER ACCOUNTS CREDIT — ACCOUNT NAME	POST. REF.	AMOUNT	CASH DEBIT
Feb 3	Q Perez		500			Supplies		500	500
5						Cash short/over		(20)	120
7				364	4300				5134
9						Capital		15,000	5000
8	K. Jones		580	324	4056			38	360
14						Cash short/over			9400
17	S. Nelson		950						950
18	K. Pitman					N/R Interest Income			200
19								32	32
21	A. Herron		590	369	4550				4914
28				439	4100	Cash short/over		(30)	580
24			1410	1400	17500				23147

PROBLEM 9.1A or 9.1B (continued)

GENERAL LEDGER

ACCOUNT ___Cash_____ ACCOUNT NO. __101__

DATE		DESCRIPTION	POST. REF.	DEBIT	CREDIT	BALANCE	
						DEBIT	CREDIT
		Balance		9960		4960	
				23194		28154	

ACCOUNT ___N/R_____ ACCOUNT NO. __109__

DATE		DESCRIPTION	POST. REF.	DEBIT	CREDIT	BALANCE	
						DEBIT	CREDIT
		Balance		800		800	

ACCOUNT ___A/R_____ ACCOUNT NO. __111__

DATE		DESCRIPTION	POST. REF.	DEBIT	CREDIT	BALANCE	
						DEBIT	CREDIT
		Balance		4075		4075	
					1910	2165	

ACCOUNT ___Supplies_____ ACCOUNT NO. __129__

DATE		DESCRIPTION	POST. REF.	DEBIT	CREDIT	BALANCE	
						DEBIT	CREDIT
		Balance		610		610	
				120		730	

ACCOUNT ___Sales Tax Payable_____ ACCOUNT NO. __231__

DATE		DESCRIPTION	POST. REF.	DEBIT	CREDIT	BALANCE	
						DEBIT	CREDIT
		Balance			205		205
					1400		1605

PROBLEM 9.1A or 9.1B (continued)

GENERAL LEDGER

ACCOUNT _____Capital_____ ACCOUNT NO. __301__

DATE	DESCRIPTION	POST. REF.	DEBIT	CREDIT	BALANCE DEBIT	BALANCE CREDIT
	Balance			34000		34000
Feb 9				15000		49000

ACCOUNT _____Sales_____ ACCOUNT NO. __401__

DATE	DESCRIPTION	POST. REF.	DEBIT	CREDIT	BALANCE DEBIT	BALANCE CREDIT
	Balance			17000		

ACCOUNT _____Intrest Income_____ ACCOUNT NO. __441__

DATE	DESCRIPTION	POST. REF.	DEBIT	CREDIT	BALANCE DEBIT	BALANCE CREDIT

ACCOUNT _____Cash Short or Over_____ ACCOUNT NO. __620__

DATE	DESCRIPTION	POST. REF.	DEBIT	CREDIT	BALANCE DEBIT	BALANCE CREDIT
			60		60	
				28	88	
			36		124	

Analyze: _____

_____

PROBLEM 9.2A or 9.2B

PAGE ___

CASH PAYMENTS JOURNAL

DATE	CK. NO.	DESCRIPTION	POST. REF.	ACCOUNTS PAYABLE DEBIT	OTHER ACCOUNTS DEBIT			PURCHASES DISCOUNT CREDIT	CASH CREDIT
					ACCOUNT NAME	POST. REF.	AMOUNT		

PROBLEM 9.2A or 9.2B (continued)

PAGE _____

PETTY CASH ANALYSIS SHEET

DATE	VOU. NO.	DESCRIPTION	RECEIPTS	PAYMENTS	DISTRIBUTION OF PAYMENTS			OTHER ACCOUNTS DEBIT	
					SUPPLIES DEBIT	DELIVERY EXPENSE DEBIT	MISC. EXPENSE DEBIT	ACCOUNT NAME	AMOUNT

Name _____

PROBLEM 9.2A or 9.2B (continued)

GENERAL LEDGER

ACCOUNT _____ ACCOUNT NO. _____

DATE	DESCRIPTION	POST. REF.	DEBIT	CREDIT	BALANCE	
					DEBIT	CREDIT

ACCOUNT _____ ACCOUNT NO. _____

DATE	DESCRIPTION	POST. REF.	DEBIT	CREDIT	BALANCE	
					DEBIT	CREDIT

ACCOUNT _____ ACCOUNT NO. _____

DATE	DESCRIPTION	POST. REF.	DEBIT	CREDIT	BALANCE	
					DEBIT	CREDIT

ACCOUNT _____ ACCOUNT NO. _____

DATE	DESCRIPTION	POST. REF.	DEBIT	CREDIT	BALANCE	
					DEBIT	CREDIT

ACCOUNT _____ ACCOUNT NO. _____

DATE	DESCRIPTION	POST. REF.	DEBIT	CREDIT	BALANCE	
					DEBIT	CREDIT

PROBLEM 9.2A or 9.2B (continued)

GENERAL LEDGER

ACCOUNT _____ ACCOUNT NO. _____

DATE	DESCRIPTION	POST. REF.	DEBIT	CREDIT	BALANCE DEBIT	CREDIT

ACCOUNT _____ ACCOUNT NO. _____

DATE	DESCRIPTION	POST. REF.	DEBIT	CREDIT	BALANCE DEBIT	CREDIT

ACCOUNT _____ ACCOUNT NO. _____

DATE	DESCRIPTION	POST. REF.	DEBIT	CREDIT	BALANCE DEBIT	CREDIT

ACCOUNT _____ ACCOUNT NO. _____

DATE	DESCRIPTION	POST. REF.	DEBIT	CREDIT	BALANCE DEBIT	CREDIT

ACCOUNT _____ ACCOUNT NO. _____

DATE	DESCRIPTION	POST. REF.	DEBIT	CREDIT	BALANCE DEBIT	CREDIT

PROBLEM 9.2A or 9.2B (continued)

GENERAL LEDGER

ACCOUNT _____ ACCOUNT NO. _____

	DATE	DESCRIPTION	POST. REF.	DEBIT	CREDIT	BALANCE	
						DEBIT	CREDIT

ACCOUNT _____ ACCOUNT NO. _____

	DATE	DESCRIPTION	POST. REF.	DEBIT	CREDIT	BALANCE	
						DEBIT	CREDIT

ACCOUNT _____ ACCOUNT NO. _____

	DATE	DESCRIPTION	POST. REF.	DEBIT	CREDIT	BALANCE	
						DEBIT	CREDIT

ACCOUNT _____ ACCOUNT NO. _____

	DATE	DESCRIPTION	POST. REF.	DEBIT	CREDIT	BALANCE	
						DEBIT	CREDIT

ACCOUNT _____ ACCOUNT NO. _____

	DATE	DESCRIPTION	POST. REF.	DEBIT	CREDIT	BALANCE	
						DEBIT	CREDIT

Analyze: _____

_____

PROBLEM 9.3A or 9.3B

SALES JOURNAL

DATE	INVOICE NO.	CUSTOMER'S NAME	POST. REF.	ACCOUNTS RECEIVABLE DR./ SALES CR.	
					1
					2
					3
					4
					5
					6
					7
					8
					9
					10
					11

CASH RECEIPTS JOURNAL

DATE	DESCRIPTION	POST. REF.	ACCOUNTS RECEIVABLE CREDIT	SALES CREDIT	OTHER ACCOUNTS CREDIT			SALES DISCOUNT DEBIT	CASH DEBIT
					ACCOUNT NAME	POST. REF.	AMOUNT		

PROBLEM 9.3A or 9.3B (continued)

GENERAL JOURNAL   PAGE _____

	DATE	DESCRIPTION	POST. REF.	DEBIT	CREDIT	
1						1
2						2
3						3
4						4
5						5
6						6
7						7
8						8
9						9
10						10
11						11
12						12

GENERAL LEDGER (PARTIAL)

ACCOUNT _____ ACCOUNT NO. _____

DATE	DESCRIPTION	POST. REF.	DEBIT	CREDIT	BALANCE	
					DEBIT	CREDIT

ACCOUNT _____ ACCOUNT NO. _____

DATE	DESCRIPTION	POST. REF.	DEBIT	CREDIT	BALANCE	
					DEBIT	CREDIT

ACCOUNT _____ ACCOUNT NO. _____

DATE	DESCRIPTION	POST. REF.	DEBIT	CREDIT	BALANCE	
					DEBIT	CREDIT

PROBLEM 9.3A or 9.3B (continued)

GENERAL LEDGER (PARTIAL)

ACCOUNT _____ ACCOUNT NO. _____

DATE	DESCRIPTION	POST. REF.	DEBIT	CREDIT	BALANCE	
					DEBIT	CREDIT

ACCOUNT _____ ACCOUNT NO. _____

DATE	DESCRIPTION	POST. REF.	DEBIT	CREDIT	BALANCE	
					DEBIT	CREDIT

ACCOUNT _____ ACCOUNT NO. _____

DATE	DESCRIPTION	POST. REF.	DEBIT	CREDIT	BALANCE	
					DEBIT	CREDIT

Analyze: _____

_____

PROBLEM 9.4A or 9.4B

PURCHASES JOURNAL   PAGE _____

DATE		PURCHASED FROM	INVOICE NUMBER	INVOICE DATE	TERMS	POST. REF.	PURCHASES DR./ ACCOUNTS PAYABLE CR.

GENERAL JOURNAL   PAGE _____

	DATE		DESCRIPTION	POST. REF.	DEBIT	CREDIT	
1							1
2							2
3							3
4							4
5							5
6							6
7							7
8							8
9							9
10							10
11							11
12							12
13							13
14							14
15							15
16							16
17							17
18							18
19							19
20							20
21							21
22							22
23							23

PROBLEM 9.4A or 9.4B (continued)

CASH PAYMENTS JOURNAL

DATE	CK. NO.	DESCRIPTION	POST. REF.	ACCOUNTS PAYABLE DEBIT	OTHER ACCOUNTS DEBIT			PURCHASES DISCOUNT CREDIT	CASH CREDIT
					ACCOUNT NAME	POST. REF.	AMOUNT		

PROBLEM 9.4A or 9.4B (continued)

GENERAL LEDGER

ACCOUNT _____ ACCOUNT NO. _____

DATE	DESCRIPTION	POST. REF.	DEBIT	CREDIT	BALANCE	
					DEBIT	CREDIT

ACCOUNT _____ ACCOUNT NO. _____

DATE	DESCRIPTION	POST. REF.	DEBIT	CREDIT	BALANCE	
					DEBIT	CREDIT

ACCOUNT _____ ACCOUNT NO. _____

DATE	DESCRIPTION	POST. REF.	DEBIT	CREDIT	BALANCE	
					DEBIT	CREDIT

ACCOUNT _____ ACCOUNT NO. _____

DATE	DESCRIPTION	POST. REF.	DEBIT	CREDIT	BALANCE	
					DEBIT	CREDIT

PROBLEM 9.4A or 9.4B (continued)

GENERAL LEDGER

ACCOUNT _____ ACCOUNT NO. _____

DATE	DESCRIPTION	POST. REF.	DEBIT	CREDIT	BALANCE	
					DEBIT	CREDIT

ACCOUNT _____ ACCOUNT NO. _____

DATE	DESCRIPTION	POST. REF.	DEBIT	CREDIT	BALANCE	
					DEBIT	CREDIT

ACCOUNT _____ ACCOUNT NO. _____

DATE	DESCRIPTION	POST. REF.	DEBIT	CREDIT	BALANCE	
					DEBIT	CREDIT

ACCOUNT _____ ACCOUNT NO. _____

DATE	DESCRIPTION	POST. REF.	DEBIT	CREDIT	BALANCE	
					DEBIT	CREDIT

ACCOUNT _____ ACCOUNT NO. _____

DATE	DESCRIPTION	POST. REF.	DEBIT	CREDIT	BALANCE	
					DEBIT	CREDIT

ACCOUNT _____ ACCOUNT NO. _____

DATE	DESCRIPTION	POST. REF.	DEBIT	CREDIT	BALANCE	
					DEBIT	CREDIT

PROBLEM 9.4A or 9.4B (continued)

Analyze: _____

EXTRA FORM

Name _____

PROBLEM 9.5A or 9.5B

_____
_____
_____

GENERAL JOURNAL   PAGE _____

	DATE		DESCRIPTION	POST. REF.	DEBIT	CREDIT	
1							1
2							2
3							3
4							4
5							5
6							6
7							7
8							8
9							9
10							10
11							11
12							12
13							13

Analyze: _____
_____

PROBLEM 9.6A or 9.6B

PROBLEM 9.6A or 9.6B (continued)

GENERAL JOURNAL   PAGE _____

	DATE		DESCRIPTION	POST. REF.	DEBIT	CREDIT	
1							1
2							2
3							3
4							4
5							5
6							6
7							7
8							8
9							9
10							10
11							11
12							12
13							13
14							14
15							15
16							16
17							17
18							18
19							19
20							20
21							21
22							22
23							23
24							24
25							25
26							26
27							27
28							28

Analyze: _____

_____

_____

_____

_____

_____

CHAPTER 9 CRITICAL THINKING PROBLEM

CHAPTER 9 CRITICAL THINKING PROBLEM (continued)

_____

Chapter 9 Practice Test Answer Key

Part A True-False

1. F	12. F
2. T	13. T
3. T	14. F
4. T	15. T
5. F	16. T
6. T	17. F
7. F	18. T
8. T	19. F
9. F	20. T
10. T	21. T
11. F	

Part B Matching

1. k
2. j
3. l
4. e
5. b
6. i
7. c
8. a
9. h
10. f
11. g
12. d

STUDY GUIDE

Understanding the Chapter

Objectives

1. Explain the major federal laws relating to employee earnings and withholding. **2.** Compute gross earnings of employees. **3.** Determine employee deductions for social security taxes. **4.** Determine employee deductions for Medicare taxes. **5.** Determine employee deductions for income taxes. **6.** Enter gross earnings, deductions, and net pay in the payroll register. **7.** Journalize payroll transactions in the general journal. **8.** Maintain an earnings record for each employee. **9.** Define the accounting terms new to this chapter.

Reading Assignment

Read Chapter 10 in the textbook. Complete the Section Self Review as you finish reading each section of the chapter, and the Comprehensive Self Review at the end of the chapter. Refer to the Chapter 10 Glossary or to the Glossary at the end of the book to find definitions for terms that are not familiar to you.

Activities

❑ **Thinking Critically**

Answer the *Thinking Critically* questions for Adobe Systems, Accounting on the Job, and Managerial Implications.

❑ **Internet Applications**

Complete the activity for Accounting on the Job.

❑ **Discussion Questions**

Answer each assigned review question in Chapter 10.

❑ **Exercises**

Complete each assigned exercise in Chapter 10. Use the forms provided in this SGWP. The objectives covered by an exercise are given after the exercise number. If you need help with an exercise, review the portion of the chapter related to the objective(s) covered.

❑ **Problems A/B**

Complete each assigned problem in Chapter 10. Use the forms provided in this SGWP. The objectives covered by a problem are given after the problem number. If you need help with a problem, review the portion of the chapter related to the objective(s) covered.

❑ **Challenge Problem**

Complete the challenge problem as assigned. Use the forms provided in this SGWP.

❑ **Critical Thinking Problem**

Complete the critical thinking problem as assigned. Use the forms provided in this SGWP.

❑ **Business Connections**

Complete the Business Connections activities as assigned to gain a deeper understanding of Chapter 10 concepts.

Practice Tests

Complete the Practice Tests, which cover the main points in your reading assignment. Compare your answers with those in the Practice Test Answer Key for Chapter 10 at the end of this chapter. If you have answered any questions incorrectly, review the related section of the text.

Part A ■ True-False *For each of the following statements, circle T in the answer column if the statement is true or F if the statement is false.*

T   F   **1.** The Medicare tax is in addition to the social security tax (FICA).

T   F   **2.** Most employers determine the amount of income tax to be withheld from the employee's pay by using withholding tables.

T   F   **3.** Employees can choose whether they want to be covered by the social security laws.

T   F   **4.** The Fair Labor Standards Act fixes a minimum wage for supervisory employees paid a monthly salary.

T   F   **5.** Payroll taxes apply to salaries and wages paid employees and to amounts paid independent contractors.

T   F   **6.** A company hires P. J. Chandy, a public accountant, to prepare monthly financial statements. Chandy comes to the company's office, reviews source documents, and later returns the statements. Chandy would be classified as an employee.

T   F   **7.** An employee worked 45 hours during the week. Her regular hourly pay is $9 per hour. Her gross pay for the week is $427.50.

T   F   **8.** The payroll register provides all the information required to make a general journal entry to record the payroll.

T   F   **9.** The workers' compensation program is a federal program.

T   F   **10.** The state unemployment tax rate can be reduced by the rate charged by the federal government in the federal unemployment tax program.

T   F   **11.** The employer is required to contribute the same amount of federal unemployment tax as the amount withheld from the employee's earnings.

T   F   **12.** The employee's marital status, number of exemptions, earnings for the pay period, and length of pay period are all factors in determining the amount of social security tax to be withheld.

STUDY GUIDE

Part B Matching *For each numbered item, choose the matching term from the box and write the identifying letter in the answer column.*

_____ 1. Time worked in excess of 40 hours per week

_____ 2. Provides for funding of retirement and disability benefits.

_____ 3. The form that employees file in order to claim the number of allowances to which they are entitled.

_____ 4. Wages before deductions

_____ 5. Wages paid in a year above the base amount subject to a tax.

_____ 6. A columnar record that shows each employee's earnings, deductions, and net pay.

_____ 7. A record for each employee showing the person's earnings and deductions for the period, along with cumulative data.

_____ 8. Deductions to pay for medical benefits for retired persons.

_____ 9. A tax levied on the employer to provide benefits to employees who lose their jobs.

_____ 10. A government publication containing withholding tables for employee taxes.

---

a. Employee earnings record

b. Payroll register

c. Exempt wages

d. Workers' compensation insurance

e. Overtime

f. Circular E

g. Medicare premiums

h. Unemployment tax

i. Federal Insurance Contributions Act

j. Employee's Withholding Allowance Certificate Form W4

k. Gross pay

Demonstration Problem

Arrow Consulting Company pays its employees monthly. Payments made by the company on November 30, 2007, follow. Cumulative amounts paid to the persons named prior to November 30 are also given.

1. John Arrow, President, gross monthly salary of $16,500; gross earnings prior to November 30, $165,000.

2. Virginia Richey, Vice President, gross monthly salary of $13,500; gross earnings paid prior to November 30, $135,000.

3. Kathryn Price, independent accountant who audits the company's accounts and performs consulting services, $17,500; gross amounts paid prior to November 30, $35,000.

4. Carolyn Wells, Treasurer, gross monthly salary of $8,000; gross earnings prior to November 30, $80,000.

5. Payment to Hankins Research Services for monthly services of Robert Hankins, a tax and financial accounting consultant, $6,000; amount paid to Hankins Research Services prior to November 30, $24,000.

Instructions

1. Use an earnings ceiling of $90,000 and a tax rate of 6.2 percent for social security taxes and a tax rate of 1.45 percent on all earnings for medicare taxes. Prepare a schedule showing:

    a. Each employee's cumulative earnings prior to November 30.

    b. Each employee's gross earnings for November.

    c. The amounts to be withheld for each payroll tax from each employee's earnings; the employee's income tax withholdings are Arrow, $5,050; Richey, $3,250; Wells, $1,175.

    d. The net amount due each employee.

    e. The total gross earnings, the total of each payroll tax deduction, and the total net amount payable to employees.

2. Give the general journal entry to record the company's payroll on November 30. Use journal page 24. Omit description.

3. Give the general journal entry to record payments to employees on November 30.

SOLUTION

EARNINGS SCHEDULE

EMPLOYEE NAME	CUMULATIVE EARNINGS	MONTHLY PAY	SOCIAL SECURITY	MEDICARE	EMPLOYEE INCOME TAX WITHHOLDING	NET PAY
John Arrow	$165,000.00	$16,500.00	—	$239.25	$5,050.00	$11,210.75
Virginia Richey	135,000.00	13,500.00	—	195.75	3,250.00	10,054.25
Carolyn Wells	80,000.00	8,000.00	496.00	116.00	1,175.00	6,213.00
Totals	$380,000.00	$38,000.00	496.00	551.00	9,475.00	$27,478.00

Kathryn Price and Robert Hankins are not employees of Arrow Consulting Company.

GENERAL JOURNAL   PAGE ___24___

	DATE		DESCRIPTION	POST. REF.	DEBIT	CREDIT	
1	2007						1
2	Nov.	30	Salaries Expense		38 0 0 0 00		2
3			Social Security Tax Payable			4 9 6 00	3
4			Medicare Tax Payable			5 5 1 00	4
5			Employee Income Tax Payable			9 4 7 5 00	5
6			Salaries Payable			27 4 7 8 00	6
7							7
8		30	Salaries Payable		27 4 7 8 00		8
9			Cash			27 4 7 8 00	9
10							10

WORKING PAPERS

Name _____

EXERCISE 10.1

EMPLOYEE NO.	HOURLY RATE	HOURS WORKED	GROSS EARNINGS
_____	_____	_____	_____
_____	_____	_____	_____
_____	_____	_____	_____
_____	_____	_____	_____

EXERCISE 10.2

EMPLOYEE NO.	HOURLY RATE	HOURS WORKED	REGULAR EARNINGS	OVERTIME EARNINGS	GROSS EARNINGS
_____	_____	_____	_____	_____	_____
_____	_____	_____	_____	_____	_____
_____	_____	_____	_____	_____	_____
_____	_____	_____	_____	_____	_____

EXERCISE 10.3

EMPLOYEE NO.	DECEMBER SALARY	EARNINGS THROUGH NOVEMBER 30	SOC. SEC. TAXABLE EARNINGS	SOCIAL SECURITY TAX
_____	_____	_____	_____	_____
_____	_____	_____	_____	_____
_____	_____	_____	_____	_____
_____	_____	_____	_____	_____

EXERCISE 10.4

EMPLOYEE NO.	DECEMBER SALARY	EARNINGS THROUGH NOVEMBER 30	MEDICARE TAXABLE EARNINGS	MEDICARE TAX
_____	_____	_____	_____	_____
_____	_____	_____	_____	_____
_____	_____	_____	_____	_____
_____	_____	_____	_____	_____

EXERCISE 10.5

EMPLOYEE NO.	MARITAL STATUS	WITHHOLDING ALLOWANCES	WEEKLY SALARY	INCOME TAX WITHHOLDING
_____	_____	_____	_____	_____
_____	_____	_____	_____	_____
_____	_____	_____	_____	_____
_____	_____	_____	_____	_____

EXERCISE 10.6

GENERAL JOURNAL   PAGE _____

	DATE		DESCRIPTION	POST. REF.	DEBIT	CREDIT	
1							1
2							2
3							3
4							4
5							5
6							6
7							7
8							8
9							9
10							10
11							11
12							12
13							13
14							14
15							15

EXERCISE 10.7

GENERAL JOURNAL   PAGE _____

	DATE		DESCRIPTION	POST. REF.	DEBIT	CREDIT	
1							1
2							2
3							3
4							4
5							5
6							6
7							7
8							8
9							9
10							10
11							11
12							12
13							13
14							14
15							15

PROBLEM 10.1A or 10.1B

EMPLOYEE NO.	HOURLY RATE	HOURS WORKED	REGULAR EARNINGS	OVERTIME EARNINGS	GROSS EARNINGS
_____	_____	_____	_____	_____	_____
_____	_____	_____	_____	_____	_____
_____	_____	_____	_____	_____	_____
_____	_____	_____	_____	_____	_____

Gross Pay _____

Social Security Tax _____

Medicare Tax _____

Income Tax Withholding _____

Health & Disability _____

United Way _____

U.S. Savings Bond _____

Net Pay _____

GENERAL JOURNAL

PAGE _____

	DATE	DESCRIPTION	POST. REF.	DEBIT	CREDIT	
1						1
2						2
3						3
4						4
5						5
6						6
7						7
8						8
9						9
10						10
11						11
12						12
13						13
14						14
15						15

Analyze: _____

_____

PROBLEM 10.2A or 10.2B

PAYROLL REGISTER   WEEK BEGINNING _____ AND ENDING _____

NAME	NO. OF ALLOW.	MARITAL STATUS	CUMULATIVE EARNINGS	NO. OF HRS.	RATE	EARNINGS			CUMULATIVE EARNINGS
						REGULAR	OVERTIME PREMIUM	GROSS AMOUNT	

PAID

TAXABLE WAGES		DEDUCTIONS						DISTRIBUTION		
SOCIAL SECURITY	MEDICARE	FUTA	SOCIAL SECURITY	MEDICARE	INCOME TAX	NET AMOUNT	CHECK NO.	THEATER WAGES	OFFICE WAGES	

PROBLEM 10.2A or 10.2B (continued)

GENERAL JOURNAL   PAGE _____

	DATE	DESCRIPTION	POST. REF.	DEBIT	CREDIT	
1						1
2						2
3						3
4						4
5						5
6						6
7						7
8						8
9						9
10						10
11						11
12						12
13						13
14						14
15						15
16						16
17						17
18						18
19						19
20						20
21						21
22						22
23						23
24						24
25						25
26						26
27						27
28						28
29						29
30						30
31						31
32						32
33						33
34						34

Analyze: _____

PROBLEM 10.3A or 10.3B

PAYROLL REGISTER   WEEK BEGINNING _____

NAME	NO. OF ALLOW.	MARITAL STATUS	CUMULATIVE EARNINGS	NO. OF HRS.	RATE	EARNINGS			CUMULATIVE EARNINGS
						REGULAR	OVERTIME PREMIUM	GROSS AMOUNT	

PAID _____ **AND ENDING** _____

TAXABLE WAGES		DEDUCTIONS						DISTRIBUTION		
SOCIAL SECURITY	MEDICARE	FUTA	SOCIAL SECURITY	MEDICARE	INCOME TAX	NET AMOUNT	CHECK NO.	OFFICE WAGES	DELIVERY WAGES

PROBLEM 10.3A or 10.3B (continued)

GENERAL JOURNAL   PAGE _____

	DATE	DESCRIPTION	POST. REF.	DEBIT	CREDIT	
1						1
2						2
3						3
4						4
5						5
6						6
7						7
8						8
9						9
10						10
11						11
12						12
13						13
14						14
15						15
16						16
17						17
18						18
19						19
20						20
21						21
22						22
23						23
24						24
25						25
26						26
27						27
28						28
29						29
30						30
31						31
32						32
33						33
34						34

Analyze: _____

_____

PROBLEM 10.4A or 10.4B

EMPLOYEE NAME	CUMULATIVE EARNINGS	MONTHLY PAY	SOCIAL SECURITY	MEDICARE	EMPLOYEE INCOME TAX WITHHOLDING	NET PAY
Totals						

GENERAL JOURNAL   PAGE _____

	DATE	DESCRIPTION	POST. REF.	DEBIT	CREDIT	
1						1
2						2
3						3
4						4
5						5
6						6
7						7
8						8
9						9
10						10
11						11
12						12
13						13
14						14
15						15
16						16
17						17
18						18
19						19
20						20
21						21
22						22
23						23
24						24
25						25
26						26

Analyze: _____

_____

CHAPTER 10 CHALLENGE PROBLEM

EMPLOYEE NAME	CUMULATIVE EARNINGS	MONTHLY PAY	SOCIAL SECURITY	MEDICARE	EMPLOYEE INCOME TAX WITHHOLDING	NET AMOUNT
____	____	____	____	____	____	____
____	____	____	____	____	____	____
____	____	____	____	____	____	____
____	____	____	____	____	____	____
____	____	____	____	____	____	____

GENERAL JOURNAL

PAGE _____

	DATE	DESCRIPTION	POST. REF.	DEBIT	CREDIT	
1						1
2						2
3						3
4						4
5						5
6						6
7						7
8						8
9						9
10						10
11						11
12						12
13						13
14						14
15						15

Analyze: _____

_____

Name _____

CHAPTER 10 CRITICAL THINKING PROBLEM

_____

_____

_____

_____

_____

_____

_____

_____

_____

_____

_____

_____

_____

_____

_____

_____

_____

_____

_____

_____

_____

Chapter 10 Practice Test Answer Key

Part A True-False	Part B Matching
1. T	1. e
2. T	2. i
3. F	3. j
4. F	4. k
5. F	5. c
6. F	6. b
7. T	7. a
8. T	8. g
9. F	9. h
10. F	10. f
11. F	
12. F	

266 ■ Chapter 10

Copyright © 2007 The McGraw-Hill Companies, Inc. All rights reserved.

Payroll Taxes, Deposits, and Reports

STUDY GUIDE

Understanding the Chapter

Objectives	**1.** Explain how and when payroll taxes are paid to the government. **2.** Compute and record the employer's social security and Medicare taxes. **3.** Record deposit of social security, Medicare, and employee income taxes. **4.** Prepare an Employer's Quarterly Federal Tax Return, Form 941. **5.** Prepare Wage and Tax Statement (Form W-2) and Annual Transmittal of Wage and Tax Statements (Form W-3). **6.** Compute and record liability for federal and state unemployment taxes and record payment of the taxes. **7.** Prepare an Employer's Federal Unemployment Tax Return, Form 940 or 940-EZ. **8.** Compute and record workers' compensation insurance premiums. **9.** Define the accounting terms new to this chapter.
Reading Assignment	Read Chapter 11 in the textbook. Complete the textbook Section Self Review as you finish reading each section of the chapter, and Comprehensive Self Review at the end of the chapter. Refer to the Chapter 11 Glossary or to the Glossary at the end of the book to find definitions for terms that are not familiar to you.

Activities

❏ **Thinking Critically**	Answer the *Thinking Critically* questions for IKEA, Computers in Accounting, and Managerial Implications.
❏ **Internet Application**	Complete the activity for Computers in Accounting.
❏ **Discussion Questions**	Answer each assigned discussion question in Chapter 11.
❏ **Exercises**	Complete each assigned exercise in Chapter 11. Use the forms provided in this SGWP. The objectives covered by an exercise are given after the exercise number. If you need help with an exercise, review the portion of the chapter related to the objective(s) covered.
❏ **Problems A/B**	Complete each assigned problem in Chapter 11. Use the forms provided in this SGWP. The objectives covered by a problem are given after the problem number. If you need help with a problem, review the portion of the chapter related to the objective(s) covered.
❏ **Challenge Problem**	Complete the challenge problem as assigned. Use the forms provided in this SGWP.
❏ **Critical Thinking Problem**	Complete the critical thinking problem as assigned. Use the forms provided in this SGWP.
❏ **Business Connections**	Complete the Business Connections activities as assigned to gain a deeper understanding of Chapter 11 concepts.

Practice Tests

Complete the Practice Tests, which cover the main points in your reading assignment. Compare your answers with those in the Practice Test Answer Key for Chapter 11 at the end of this chapter. If you have answered any questions incorrectly, review the related section of the text.

Part A True-False *For each of the following statements, circle T in the answer column if the statement is true or F if the statement is false.*

T   F   1. A business firm pays income tax withholding at the same rate and on the same taxable wages as employees.

T   F   2. The employer's payroll taxes are usually recorded at the end of each payroll period, even though the cash will not be paid out until later.

T   F   3. Most states allow a credit against the SUTA for amounts paid to the federal government as FUTA.

T   F   4. The federal government grants a lower federal unemployment rate under an experience rating system to those employers who provide stable employment.

T   F   5. Under a typical state plan, the federal government actually receives 0.6 percent of the taxable wages because the employer is allowed credits for payments made to the state.

T   F   6. The federal unemployment tax for the year is based on an audit of the payroll for the year.

T   F   7. Premiums on workers' compensation insurance vary with the type of work performed by employees.

T   F   8. The premium on workers' compensation insurance is based on the federal unemployment tax.

T   F   9. The credit against the federal unemployment tax is the amount actually paid to the state under its unemployment compensation insurance program.

T   F   10. Employers with a small number of employees are frequently required to deposit the entire amount of estimated workers' compensation insurance premiums early in the year.

T   F   11. The base for the state unemployment tax may be greater than the base for federal unemployment tax.

T   F   12. Each employer subject to the Federal Unemployment Compensation Tax Act must file an annual return on Form 940 by January 15 of the following year.

T   F   13. The employee must attach a Form W-3 to his or her federal income tax return.

T   F   14. Payments of social security tax, Medicare tax, and employee income tax withheld for a year may be deposited without penalty in an authorized depository at any time up to January 31 of the following year.

T   F   15. Only the amount of each employee's earnings up to $7,000 each year is subject to Medicare tax.

T   F   16. Employees' individual earnings records provide much of the information needed to prepare the Employer's Quarterly Federal Tax Return, Form 941.

T   F   17. On each date of payment of an employee's wages, the employer must provide the employee with a statement, on Form W-2, of earnings and taxes withheld.

T   F   18. During the month immediately following the close of each calendar quarter, an employer is required to file a quarterly tax report and pay in or deposit any balance owed for social security and Medicare taxes and employees' income tax withheld.

Part B Matching

For each number item, choose the matching term from the box and write the identifying letter in the answer column.

_____ 1. A tax borne equally by the employer and employee.

_____ 2. A tax paid solely by the employer.

_____ 3. An IRS publication containing tax rates and other information about payroll taxes.

_____ 4. Plan providing benefits to employees who are injured or become ill on the job.

_____ 5. A plan under which the SUTA is adjusted to reflect the unemployment experience of the employer.

_____ 6. A deposit "coupon" accompanying the employer's deposit of taxes in a commercial bank.

_____ 7. An annual report to the federal government summarizing the employer's unemployment compensation tax for the year.

_____ 8. A quarterly report to the federal government summarizing taxable wages and payroll taxes due for the quarter.

_____ 9. A yearly form sent to the U.S. government summarizing earnings and payroll taxes withheld for the year.

_____ 10. A statement of earnings and deductions for each employee.

a. Workers' compensation
b. Form 8109
c. Form 941
d. Form 940
e. Form W-3
f. Form W-2
g. Experience rating system
h. Publication 15, Circular E
i. Federal unemployment tax
j. Medicare tax

Demonstration Problem

The payroll register of the Quick Copy Center showed employee earnings of $12,960 for the month ended January 31, 2007. Employee income tax withholding was $3,500. Tax rates are: social security, 6.2 percent, and Medicare, 1.45 percent.

Instructions

1. Compute the employees' social security and Medicare taxes.

2. Record the payroll for January in the general journal, page 4.

3. Compute the employer's payroll taxes for the period.

4. Prepare a general journal entry to record the employer's payroll taxes for the period.

5. Prepare a general journal entry to record the February 5 deposit of the social security, Medicare, and employee income taxes for the month.

SOLUTION

CALCULATION OF EMPLOYEE TAXES

Social security: 0.062 × $12,960	$803.52
Medicare: 0.0145 × $12,960	187.92
	$991.44

CALCULATION OF EMPLOYER TAXES

Social security: 0.062 × $12,960	$803.52
Medicare: 0.0145 × $12,960	187.92
	$991.44

SOLUTION (continued)

GENERAL JOURNAL   PAGE _____ 3 _____

	DATE		DESCRIPTION	POST. REF.	DEBIT	CREDIT	
1	2007						1
2	Jan.	31	Salaries Expense		1 2 9 6 0 00		2
3			Social Security Tax Payable			8 0 3 52	3
4			Medicare Tax Payable			1 8 7 92	4
5			Employee Income Tax Payable			3 5 0 0 00	5
6			Salaries Payable			8 4 6 8 56	6
7			Payroll for January				7
8							8
9		31	Payroll Tax Expense		9 9 1 44		9
10			Social Security Tax Payable			8 0 3 52	10
11			Medicare Tax Payable			1 8 7 92	11
12			Payroll for January				12
13							13
14	Feb.	5	Social Security Tax Payable		1 6 0 7 04		14
15			Medicare Tax Payable		3 7 5 84		15
16			Employee Income Tax Payable		3 5 0 0 00		16
17			Cash			5 4 8 2 88	17
18			Deposit of payroll taxes withholding				18
19							19
20							20
21							21
22							22
23							23
24							24
25							25
26							26
27							27
28							28
29							29
30							30
31							31
32							32
33							33
34							34
35							35
36							36
37							37
38							38

WORKING PAPERS

Name _____

EXERCISE 11.1

_____

_____

_____

_____

EXERCISE 11.2

GENERAL JOURNAL   PAGE _____

	DATE	DESCRIPTION	POST. REF.	DEBIT	CREDIT	
1						1
2						2
3						3
4						4
5						5
6						6
7						7

EXERCISE 11.3

TAX	BASE	RATE	AMOUNT
_____	_____	_____	_____
_____	_____	_____	_____
_____	_____	_____	_____
_____	_____	_____	_____
_____	_____	_____	_____

EXERCISE 11.4

GENERAL JOURNAL   PAGE _____

	DATE	DESCRIPTION	POST. REF.	DEBIT	CREDIT	
1						1
2						2
3						3
4						4
5						5
6						6
7						7

EXERCISE 11.5

_____

_____

_____

EXERCISE 11.6

GENERAL JOURNAL

PAGE _____

	DATE		DESCRIPTION	POST. REF.	DEBIT	CREDIT	
1							1
2							2
3							3
4							4
5							5
6							6
7							7

EXERCISE 11.7

_____

_____

_____

_____

EXERCISE 11.8

WORK CLASSIFICATION	ESTIMATED EARNINGS	RATE	ESTIMATED PREMIUM
_____	_____	_____	_____
_____	_____	_____	_____
_____	_____	_____	_____

PROBLEM 11.1A or 11.1B

TAX	BASE	RATE	AMOUNT
_____	_____	_____	_____
_____	_____	_____	_____
_____	_____	_____	_____
_____	_____	_____	_____
_____	_____	_____	_____
_____	_____	_____	_____

GENERAL JOURNAL

PAGE __28__

	DATE	DESCRIPTION	POST. REF.	DEBIT	CREDIT	
1						1
2						2
3						3
4						4
5						5
6						6
7						7
8						8
9						9
10						10
11						11
12						12

Analyze: _____

_____

PROBLEM 11.2A or 11.2B

GENERAL JOURNAL   PAGE _____

	DATE		DESCRIPTION	POST. REF.	DEBIT	CREDIT	
1							1
2							2
3							3
4							4
5							5
6							6
7							7
8							8
9							9
10							10
11							11
12							12
13							13
14							14
15							15
16							16
17							17
18							18
19							19
20							20
21							21
22							22
23							23
24							24
25							25
26							26
27							27
28							28
29							29
30							30
31							31
32							32
33							33

Analyze: _____

_____

Name _____

PROBLEM 11.3A or 11.3B

GENERAL JOURNAL   PAGE _____

	DATE	DESCRIPTION	POST. REF.	DEBIT	CREDIT	
1						1
2						2
3						3
4						4
5						5
6						6
7						7
8						8
9						9
10						10
11						11
12						12
13						13
14						14
15						15
16						16
17						17
18						18
19						19
20						20
21						21
22						22
23						23
24						24
25						25
26						26
27						27
28						28
29						29
30						30
31						31
32						32
33						33

Analyze: _____

_____

PROBLEM 11.3A or 11.3B (continued)

Form **941 for 2007:** Employer's Quarterly Federal Tax Return

9901

(Rev. January 2005)

Department of the Treasury — Internal Revenue Service

OMB No. 1545-0029

Employer identification number ☐☐ – ☐☐☐☐☐☐☐

Name (not your trade name) _____

Trade name (if any) _____

Address _____

Number   Street   Suite or room number

_____

City   State   ZIP code

☐ **1:** January, February, March

☐ **2:** April, May, June

☐ **3:** July, August, September

☐ **4:** October, November, December

Read the separate instructions before you fill out this form. Please type or print within the boxes.

1 Number of employees who received wages, tips, or other compensation for the pay period including: *Mar. 12* (Quarter 1), *June 12* (Quarter 2), *Sept. 12* (Quarter 3), *Dec. 12* (Quarter 4)   **1** ☐

2 Wages, tips, and other compensation . . . .   **2** ☐

3 Total income tax withheld from wages, tips, and other compensation   **3** ☐

4 If no wages, tips, and other compensation are subject to social security or Medicare tax .   ☐ Check and go to line 6.

5 Taxable social security and Medicare wages and tips:

	Column 1		Column 2
5a Taxable social security wages	☐	× .124 =	☐
5b Taxable social security tips	☐	× .124 =	☐
5c Taxable Medicare wages & tips	☐	× .029 =	☐

5d Total social security and Medicare taxes (*Column 2*, lines 5a + 5b + 5c = line 5d)   **5d** ☐

6 Total taxes before adjustments (lines 3 + 5d = line 6) . . . .   **6** ☐

7 Tax adjustments (If your answer is a negative number, write it in brackets.):

7a Current quarter's fractions of cents . . . .   ☐

7b Current quarter's sick pay . . . .   ☐

7c Current quarter's adjustments for tips and group-term life insurance   ☐

7d Current year's income tax withholding (Attach Form 941c) . .   ☐

7e Prior quarters' social security and Medicare taxes (Attach Form 941c)   ☐

7f Special additions to federal income tax (reserved use) . . . .   ☐

7g Special additions to social security and Medicare (reserved use)   ☐

7h Total adjustments (Combine all amounts: lines 7a through 7g.) . . . . .   **7h** ☐

8 Total taxes after adjustments (Combine lines 6 and 7h.) . . . .   **8** ☐

9 Advance earned income credit (EIC) payments made to employees . . . . . .   **9** ☐

10 Total taxes after adjustment for advance EIC (lines 8 – 9 = line 10) . . . . .   **10** ☐

11 Total deposits for this quarter, including overpayment applied from a prior quarter . .   **11** ☐

12 Balance due (lines 10 – 11 = line 12) Make checks payable to the *United States Treasury* .   **12** ☐

13 Overpayment (If line 11 is more than line 10, write the difference here.) ☐   Check one ☐ Apply to next return.

☐ Send a refund.

For Privacy Act and Paperwork Reduction Act Notice, see the back of the Payment Voucher.   Cat. No. 17001Z   Form **941**

Name _____

PROBLEM 11.3A or 11.3B (continued)

9902

Name (not your trade name)	Employer identification number

If you are unsure about whether you are a monthly schedule depositor or a semiweekly schedule depositor, see *Pub. 15 (Circular E), section 11.*

14 ☐☐ Write the state abbreviation for the state where you made your deposits OR write "MU" if you made your deposits in *multiple* states.

15 Check one: ☐ Line 10 is less than $2,500. Go to Part 3.

☐ You were a monthly schedule depositor for the entire quarter. Fill out your tax liability for each month. Then go to Part 3.

Tax liability: Month 1 [.]

Month 2 [.]

Month 3 [.]

Total [.] Total must equal line 10.

☐ You were a semiweekly schedule depositor for any part of this quarter. Fill out *Schedule B (Form 941): Report of Tax Liability for Semiweekly Schedule Depositors,* and attach it to this form.

16 If your business has closed and you do not have to file returns in the future . . . . ☐ Check here, and

enter the final date you paid wages [/ /] .

17 If you are a seasonal employer and you do not have to file a return for every quarter of the year . ☐ Check here.

Do you want to allow an employee, a paid tax preparer, or another person to discuss this return with the IRS? See the instructions for details.

☐ Yes. Designee's name [ ]

Phone ( ) – Personal Identification Number (PIN) ☐☐☐☐☐

☐ No.

Under penalties of perjury, I declare that I have examined this return, including accompanying schedules and statements, and to the best of my knowledge and belief, it is true, correct, and complete.

X

Sign your name here [ ]

Print name and title [ ]

Date [/ /] Phone ( ) –

Preparer's signature [ ]

Firm's name [ ]

Address [ ] EIN [ ]

[ ] ZIP code [ ]

Date [/ /] Phone ( ) – SSN/PTIN [ ]

☐ Check if you are self-employed.

Form **941**

PROBLEM 11.4A or 11.4B

_____

_____

_____

GENERAL JOURNAL   PAGE _____

	DATE	DESCRIPTION	POST. REF.	DEBIT	CREDIT	
1						1
2						2
3						3
4						4
5						5
6						6
7						7
8						8
9						9
10						10
11						11
12						12
13						13
14						14
15						15
16						16
17						17
18						18
19						19
20						20
21						21
22						22
23						23
24						24
25						25
26						26
27						27
28						28
29						29

Analyze: _____

_____

PROBLEM 11.5A or 11.5B

GENERAL JOURNAL   PAGE _____

	DATE	DESCRIPTION	POST. REF.	DEBIT	CREDIT	
1						1
2						2
3						3
4						4
5						5
6						6
7						7
8						8
9						9
10						10
11						11
12						12
13						13
14						14
15						15
16						16
17						17
18						18
19						19
20						20
21						21
22						22
23						23
24						24
25						25
26						26
27						27
28						28
29						29
30						30
31						31
32						32
33						33
34						34

Analyze: _____

_____

PROBLEM 11.5A or 11.5B (continued)

Form 940-EZ

Department of the Treasury
Internal Revenue Service   (99)

Employer's Annual Federal Unemployment (FUTA) Tax Return

▶ See the separate Instructions for Form 940-EZ for information on completing this form.

OMB No. 1545-1110

2007

T	
FF	
FD	
FP	
I	
T	

You must complete this section. ▶

Name (as distinguished from trade name)

Trade name, if any

Address (number and street)

Calendar year

Employer identification number (EIN)

City, state, and ZIP code

*Answer the questions under **Who May Use Form 940-EZ** on page 2. If you cannot use Form 940-EZ, you must use Form 940.*

A Enter the amount of contributions paid to your state unemployment fund (see the separate instructions) . ▶ $ _____

B (1) Enter the name of the state where you have to pay contributions . . . . ▶ _____

  (2) Enter your state reporting number as shown on your state unemployment tax return ▶

If you will not have to file returns in the future, check here (see **Who Must File** in separate instructions) **and complete and sign the return.** ▶ ☐

If this is an Amended Return, check here (see **Amended Returns** in the separate instructions) . . . . ▶ ☐

Taxable Wages and FUTA Tax

1	Total payments (including payments shown on lines 2 and 3) during the calendar year for services of employees	**1**	
2	Exempt payments. (Explain all exempt payments, attaching additional sheets if necessary.) ▶ _____	**2**	
3	Payments of more than $7,000 for services. Enter only amounts over the first $7,000 paid to each employee **(see the separate instructions)**	**3**	
4	Add lines 2 and 3	**4**	
5	**Total taxable wages** (subtract line 4 from line 1) . . . . ▶	**5**	
6	FUTA tax. Multiply the wages on line 5 by .008 and enter here. **(If the result is over $100, also complete Part II.)**	**6**	
7	Total FUTA tax deposited for the year, including any overpayment applied from a prior year	**7**	
8	**Balance due** (subtract line 7 from line 6). Pay to the "United States Treasury." . . . . ▶	**8**	
	If you owe more than $100, see **Depositing FUTA tax** in the separate instructions.		
9	**Overpayment** (subtract line 6 from line 7). Check if it is to be: ☐ **Applied to next return** or ☐ **Refunded** ▶	**9**	

Record of Quarterly Federal Unemployment Tax Liability (Do not include state liability.) Complete only if line 6 is over $100.

Quarter	First (Jan. 1 – Mar. 31)	Second (Apr. 1 – June 30)	Third (July 1 – Sept. 30)	Fourth (Oct. 1 – Dec. 31)	Total for year
Liability for quarter					

Third–Party Designee	Do you want to allow another person to discuss this return with the IRS (see the separate instructions)? ☐ **Yes.** Complete the following. ☐ **No**		
	Designee's name ▶	Phone no. ▶ ( )	Personal identification number (PIN) ▶

Under penalties of perjury, I declare that I have examined this return, including accompanying schedules and statements, and, to the best of my knowledge and belief, it is true, correct, and complete, and that no part of any payment made to a state unemployment fund claimed as a credit was, or is to be, deducted from the payments to employees.

Signature ▶ _____ Title (Owner, etc.) ▶ _____ Date ▶ _____

For Privacy Act and Paperwork Reduction Act Notice, see the separate instructions.   ▼ **DETACH HERE** ▼   Cat. No. 10983G   Form **940-EZ**

Form 940-V(EZ)

Department of the Treasury
Internal Revenue Service

Payment Voucher

Use this voucher only when making a payment with your return.

OMB No. 1545-1110

2007

Complete boxes 1, 2, and 3. Do not send cash, and do not staple your payment to this voucher. Make your check or money order payable to the "United States Treasury." Be sure to enter your employer identification number (EIN), "Form 940-EZ," and "2004" on your payment.

1 Enter your employer identification number (EIN).	**2**		Dollars	Cents
	Enter the amount of your payment. ▶			
	3 Enter your business name (individual name for sole proprietors).			
	Enter your address.			
	Enter your city, state, and ZIP code.			

PROBLEM 11.6A or 11.6B

WORK CLASSIFICATION	ESTIMATED EARNINGS	INSURANCE RATE	ESTIMATED PREMIUMS
_____	_____	_____	_____
_____	_____	_____	_____
_____	_____	_____	_____
_____	_____	_____	_____

WORK CLASSIFICATION	ACTUAL EARNINGS	INSURANCE RATE	ACTUAL PREMIUMS
_____	_____	_____	_____
_____	_____	_____	_____
_____	_____	_____	_____
_____	_____	_____	_____
_____	_____	_____	_____

PROBLEM 11.6A or 11.6B (continued)

GENERAL JOURNAL   PAGE _____

	DATE		DESCRIPTION	POST. REF.	DEBIT	CREDIT	
1							1
2							2
3							3
4							4
5							5
6							6
7							7
8							8
9							9
10							10
11							11
12							12
13							13
14							14
15							15
16							16
17							17
18							18
19							19

Analyze: _____

_____

CHAPTER 11 CHALLENGE PROBLEM

1. _____

_____

2. _____

_____

3. _____

_____

4. _____

_____

5. _____

_____

Analyze: _____

_____

CHAPTER 11 CRITICAL THINKING PROBLEM

1. _____

_____

_____

_____

2. YEARLY COST—CURRENT SYSTEM

_____

_____

_____

_____

_____

_____

_____

_____

_____

_____

_____

_____

_____

_____

_____

CHAPTER 11 CRITICAL THINKING PROBLEM (continued)

YEARLY COST—PROPOSED SYSTEM

_____
_____
_____
_____
_____
_____
_____
_____
_____
_____
_____
_____
_____
_____

3. _____
_____
_____
_____
_____

Chapter 11 Practice Test Answer Key

Part A True-False		Part B Matching
1. F	10. T	1. j
2. T	11. T	2. i
3. F	12. F	3. h
4. F	13. F	4. a
5. F	14. F	5. g
6. F	15. F	6. b
7. T	16. T	7. d
8. F	17. F	8. c
9. F	18. T	9. e
		10. f

CHAPTER 12 / Accruals, Deferrals, and the Worksheet

STUDY GUIDE

Understanding the Chapter

Objectives

1. Determine the adjustment for merchandise inventory and enter the adjustment on the worksheet. **2.** Compute adjustments for accrued and prepaid expense items and enter the adjustments on the worksheet. **3.** Compute adjustments for accrued and deferred income items and enter the adjustments on the worksheet. **4.** Complete a ten-column worksheet. **5.** Define the accounting terms new to this chapter.

Reading Assignment

Read Chapter 12 in the textbook. Complete the textbook Section Self Review as you finish reading each section of the chapter, and the Comprehensive Self Review at the end of the chapter. Refer to the Chapter 12 Glossary or to the Glossary at the end of the book to find definitions for terms that are not familiar to you.

Activities

❏ **Thinking Critically**

Answer the Part 4 *Thinking Critically* question for Johnson & Johnson. Answer the *Thinking Critically* questions for American Eagle Outfitters, Accounting on the Job, and Managerial Implications.

❏ **Internet Application**

Complete the activity for Accounting on the Job.

❏ **Discussion Questions**

Answer each assigned discussion question in Chapter 12.

❏ **Exercises**

Complete each assigned exercise in Chapter 12. Use the forms provided in this SGWP. The objectives covered by an exercise are given after the exercise number. If you need help with an exercise, review the portion of the chapter related to the objective(s) covered.

❏ **Problems A/B**

Complete each assigned problem in Chapter 12. Use the forms provided in this SGWP. The objectives covered by a problem are given after the problem number. If you need help with a problem, review the portion of the chapter related to the objective(s) covered.

❏ **Challenge Problem**

Complete the challenge problem as assigned. Use the forms provided in this SGWP.

❏ **Critical Thinking Problem**

Complete the critical thinking problem as assigned. Use the forms provided in this SGWP.

❏ **Business Connections**

Complete the Business Connections activities as assigned to gain a deeper understanding of Chapter 12 concepts.

Practice Tests

Complete the Practice Tests, which cover the main points in your reading assignment. Compare your answers with those in the Practice Test Answer Key for Chapter 12 at the end of this chapter. If you have answered any questions incorrectly, review the related section of the text.

Part A True-False *For each of the following statements, circle T in the answer column if the statement is true or F if the statement is false.*

T F **1.** It is not necessary to adjust the accounts when preparing monthly or quarterly statements.

T F **2.** A prepaid expense incorrectly charged to expense in an accounting period results in an understatement of net income in that period and an overstatement of net income in the following period.

T F **3.** In preparing financial statements, it is unnecessary to make adjustments for relatively small items because they are immaterial and will not affect the statements.

T F **4.** Accrued income has been earned but not recorded, while deferred income has been recorded but not earned.

T F **5.** The entry to record accrued interest on notes payable is a credit to **Interest Payable** and a debit to **Interest Expense.**

T F **6. Interest Receivable** is usually classified as a revenue account.

T F **7.** In most cases, **Prepaid Interest Expense** will be classified as a current liability on the balance sheet.

T F **8.** The **Interest Expense** account must be adjusted if an interest-bearing note payable is outstanding at the end of the fiscal period and interest has not been paid on that date.

T F **9.** Under the accrual basis of accounting, purchases are recorded when the title to the goods passes to the buyer.

T F **10.** In the "adjustments" column of the worksheet, the **Merchandise Inventory** is debited for the amount of ending inventory and credited for the amount of beginning inventory.

T F **11.** The **Unearned Subscriptions Income** account will appear in the Assets section of the balance sheet.

T F **12.** The trial balance figures for accumulated depreciation accounts do not contain the depreciation for the current period.

T F **13.** At the end of an accounting period, an adjustment is needed to record as an expense any part of the balance in an asset account that has been used up or has expired.

T F **14.** On the trial balance, the **Store Supplies** account shows a debit balance of $300. A physical count showed supplies on hand of $80. The adjusting entry includes a debit of $80 to the **Store Supplies Expense** account.

T F **15.** An adjustment for depreciation results in an entry debiting the **Depreciation Expense** account and crediting the **Accumulated Depreciation** account.

T F **16.** Office or store supplies that have been paid for in cash do not need any adjusting entries.

T F **17.** The net income for the business is entered as a debit entry in the Balance Sheet section and as a credit entry in the Income Statement section of the worksheet.

T F **18.** The accountant completes the worksheet and prepares the financial statements as soon as all adjustments have been entered on the worksheet.

T F **19.** The Adjusted Trial Balance column of the worksheet tests only the arithmetic accuracy of the worksheet to that point in the worksheet and statement preparation process.

T F **20.** After the amounts shown in the Adjusted Trial Balance section have been extended the difference between the total debits and total credits in the balance sheet section represents the net income or loss for the period.

T F **21.** Adjusting entries are recorded in the general journal after the worksheet and the financial statements are completed.

T F **22.** The beginning merchandise inventory does not appear in the Adjusted Trial Balance.

T F **23.** The **Drawing** account balance is extended to the Debit column in the Income Statement section.

T F **24.** The statement of owner's equity should be prepared before the income statement is prepared.

T F **25.** The financial statements are prepared directly from the worksheet.

Part B Exercise *In each of the following independent cases give the general journal entry to adjust the accounts for the year on December 31, 2007. Omit the descriptions.*

1. Store supplies costing $1,250 were purchased during the year and were charged to the **Store Supplies** account. At the end of the year, supplies costing $250 were on hand.

GENERAL JOURNAL   PAGE_____

	DATE	DESCRIPTION	POST. REF.	DEBIT	CREDIT	
1						1
2						2

2. On December 1, 2007 the company gave a $4,000 note payable to a supplier. The note bears interest at 6 percent.

GENERAL JOURNAL   PAGE_____

	DATE	DESCRIPTION	POST. REF.	DEBIT	CREDIT	
1						1
2						2

3. On November 1, 2004, the company received a four-month, 12 percent note for $1,500 from settlement of an overdue account. No interest has been recorded on the note.

GENERAL JOURNAL   PAGE_____

	DATE	DESCRIPTION	POST. REF.	DEBIT	CREDIT	
1						1
2						2

4. On October 1, 2007, the company purchased a one-year insurance policy for $1,520. The amount was charged to **Prepaid Insurance.**

GENERAL JOURNAL   PAGE_____

	DATE	DESCRIPTION	POST. REF.	DEBIT	CREDIT	
1						1
2						2

Demonstration Problem

The trial balance for Peggy's Imports on December 31, 2007, the end of its accounting period, is shown on the worksheet.

Instructions

1. Complete the worksheet for the year, using the following information:
   - **a-b.** Ending merchandise inventory, $107,170.
   - **c.** Uncollectible accounts expense, $750.
   - **d.** Supplies on hand December 31, 2007, $680.
   - **e.** Depreciation on store equipment, $8,030.
   - **f.** Depreciation on office equipment, $2,950.
   - **g.** Accrued sales salaries, $4,000; accrued office salaries, $750.
   - **h.** Tax on accrued salaries: social security, $294.50; Medicare, $68.88.

2. Journalize the adjusting entries on page 15 of the general journal.

Peggy's Imports

Worksheet

December 31, 2007

	ACCOUNT NAME	TRIAL BALANCE DEBIT	TRIAL BALANCE CREDIT	ADJUSTMENTS DEBIT	ADJUSTMENTS CREDIT
1	Cash	9 8 1 0 00			
2	Accounts Receivable	32 3 4 0 00			
3	Allowance for Doubtful Accounts		5 0 6 0 00		(c) 7 5 0 00
4	Merchandise Inventory	116 7 8 0 00		(b)107 1 7 0 00	(a)116 7 8 0 00
5	Supplies	10 6 0 0 00			(d) 9 9 2 0 00
6	Store Equipment	84 0 0 0 00			
7	Accumulated Depreciation—Store Equip.		16 5 9 0 00		(e) 8 0 3 0 00
8	Office Equipment	25 7 0 0 00			
9	Accumulated Depreciation—Office Equip.		7 0 3 3 00		(f) 2 9 5 0 00
10	Accounts Payable		22 5 6 0 00		
11	Salaries Payable				(g) 4 7 5 0 00
12	Social Security Tax Payable				(h) 2 9 4 50
13	Medicare Tax Payable				(h) 6 8 88
14	Peggy Culey, Capital		230 7 6 4 00		
15	Peggy Culey, Drawing	26 0 0 0 00			
16	Income Summary			(a)116 7 8 0 00	(b)107 1 7 0 00
17	Sales		394 6 4 2 00		
18	Sales Returns and Allowances	8 1 5 5 00			
19	Purchases	197 5 3 4 00			
20	Purchase Returns and Allowances		1 2 0 0 00		
21	Purchase Discounts		6 0 0 00		
22	Freight In	12 2 6 0 00			
23	Sales Salaries Expense	94 5 8 0 00		(g) 4 0 0 0 00	
24	Rent Expense	31 0 0 0 00			
25	Advertising Expense	12 0 4 5 00			
26	Supplies Expense			(d) 9 9 2 0 00	
27	Depreciation Expense—Store Equipment			(e) 8 0 3 0 00	
28	Office Salaries Expense	17 6 4 5 00		(g) 7 5 0 00	
29	Payroll Taxes Expense			(h) 3 6 3 38	
30	Depreciation Expense—Office Equipment			(f) 2 9 5 0 00	
31	Uncollectible Accounts Expense			(c) 7 5 0 00	
32		678 4 4 9 00	678 4 4 9 00	250 7 1 3 38	250 7 1 3 38
33	Net Loss				
34					
35					

SOLUTION (continued)

ADJUSTED TRIAL BALANCE		INCOME STATEMENT		BALANCE SHEET		
DEBIT	CREDIT	DEBIT	CREDIT	DEBIT	CREDIT	
9 8 1 0 00				9 8 1 0 00		1
32 3 4 0 00				32 3 4 0 00		2
	5 8 1 0 00				5 8 1 0 00	3
107 1 7 0 00				107 1 7 0 00		4
6 8 0 00				6 8 0 00		5
84 0 0 0 00				84 0 0 0 00		6
	24 6 2 0 00				24 6 2 0 00	7
25 7 0 0 00				25 7 0 0 00		8
	9 9 8 3 00				9 9 8 3 00	9
	22 5 6 0 00				22 5 6 0 00	10
	4 7 5 0 00				4 7 5 0 00	11
	2 9 4 50				2 9 4 50	12
	6 8 88				6 8 88	13
	230 7 6 4 00				230 7 6 4 00	14
26 0 0 0 00				26 0 0 0 00		15
116 7 8 0 00	107 1 7 0 00	116 7 8 0 00	107 1 7 0 00			16
	394 6 4 2 00		394 6 4 2 00			17
8 1 5 5 00		8 1 5 5 00				18
197 5 3 4 00		197 5 3 4 00				19
	1 2 0 0 00		1 2 0 0 00			20
	6 0 0 00		6 0 0 00			21
12 2 6 0 00		12 2 6 0 00				22
98 5 8 0 00		98 5 8 0 00				23
31 0 0 0 00		31 0 0 0 00				24
12 0 4 5 00		12 0 4 5 00				25
9 9 2 0 00		9 9 2 0 00				26
8 0 3 0 00		8 0 3 0 00				27
18 3 9 5 00		18 3 9 5 00				28
3 6 3 38		3 6 3 38				29
2 9 5 0 00		2 9 5 0 00				30
7 5 0 00		7 5 0 00				31
802 4 6 2 38	802 4 6 2 38	516 7 6 2 38	503 6 1 2 00	285 7 0 0 00	298 8 5 0 38	32
			13 1 5 0 38	13 1 5 0 38		33
		516 7 6 2 38	516 7 6 2 38	298 8 5 0 38	298 8 5 0 38	34
						35

SOLUTION (continued)

GENERAL JOURNAL PAGE __15__

	DATE		DESCRIPTION	POST. REF.	DEBIT	CREDIT	
1	2007						1
2			(a)				2
3	Dec.	31	Income Summary		116 7 8 0 00		3
4			Merchandise Inventory			116 7 8 0 00	4
5			Close beginning merchandise inventory				5
6			(b)				6
7		31	Merchandise Inventory		107 1 7 0 00		7
8			Income Summary			107 1 7 0 00	8
9			Record ending merchandise inventory				9
10			(c)				10
11		31	Uncollectible Accounts Expense		7 5 0 00		11
12			Allowance for Doubtful Accounts			7 5 0 00	12
13			Record estimated uncollectible accounts expense				13
14			(d)				14
15		31	Supplies Expense		9 9 2 0 00		15
16			Supplies			9 9 2 0 00	16
17			Record supplies used during year				17
18			(e)				18
19		31	Depreciation Expense—Store Equipment		8 0 3 0 00		19
20			Accumulated Depreciation—Store Equipment			8 0 3 0 00	20
21			Record depreciation on store equipment for year				21
22			(f)				22
23		31	Depreciation Expense—Office Equipment		2 9 5 0 00		23
24			Accumulated Depreciation—Office Equipment			2 9 5 0 00	24
25			Record depreciation on office equipment for year				25
26			(g)				26
27		31	Sales Salaries Expense		4 0 0 0 00		27
28			Office Salaries Expense		7 5 0 00		28
29			Salaries Payable			4 7 5 0 00	29
30			Record accrued salaries				30
31			(h)				31
32		31	Payroll Taxes Expense		3 6 3 38		32
33			Social Security Tax Payable			2 9 4 50	33
34			Medicare Tax Payable			6 8 88	34
35			Record accrued payroll taxes				35
36							36

WORKING PAPERS

Name _____

EXERCISE 12.1

GENERAL JOURNAL

PAGE _____

	DATE	DESCRIPTION	POST. REF.	DEBIT	CREDIT	
1						1
2						2
3						3
4						4
5						5
6						6
7						7

EXERCISE 12.2

_____

_____

_____

EXERCISE 12.3

GENERAL JOURNAL

PAGE _____

	DATE	DESCRIPTION	POST. REF.	DEBIT	CREDIT	
1						1
2						2
3						3
4						4
5						5
6						6
7						7
8						8
9						9
10						10
11						11
12						12
13						13
14						14
15						15
16						16
17						17
18						18

EXERCISE 12.4

GENERAL JOURNAL   PAGE _____

	DATE	DESCRIPTION	POST. REF.	DEBIT	CREDIT	
1						1
2						2
3						3
4						4
5						5
6						6
7						7
8						8
9						9
10						10
11						11
12						12
13						13

EXERCISE 12.5

GENERAL JOURNAL   PAGE _____

	DATE	DESCRIPTION	POST. REF.	DEBIT	CREDIT	
1						1
2						2
3						3
4						4
5						5
6						6
7						7
8						8

EXERCISE 12.6

GENERAL JOURNAL   PAGE _____

	DATE	DESCRIPTION	POST. REF.	DEBIT	CREDIT	
1						1
2						2
3						3
4						4

EXERCISE 12.7

GENERAL JOURNAL   PAGE _____

	DATE	DESCRIPTION	POST. REF.	DEBIT	CREDIT	
1						1
2						2
3						3
4						4
5						5
6						6
7						7
8						8
9						9
10						10
11						11
12						12
13						13

PROBLEM 12.1A or 12.1B

GENERAL JOURNAL   PAGE ____1____

	DATE		DESCRIPTION	POST. REF.	DEBIT	CREDIT	
1							1
2							2
3							3
4							4
5							5
6							6
7							7
8							8
9							9
10							10
11							11
12							12
13							13
14							14
15							15
16							16
17							17
18							18
19							19
20							20
21							21
22							22
23							23
24							24
25							25
26							26
27							27
28							28
29							29
30							30
31							31
32							32
33							33
34							34
35							35
36							36
37							37

PROBLEM 12.1A or 12.1B (continued)

GENERAL JOURNAL   PAGE ___2___

	DATE		DESCRIPTION	POST. REF.	DEBIT	CREDIT	
1							1
2							2
3							3
4							4
5							5
6							6
7							7
8							8
9							9
10							10
11							11
12							12
13							13
14							14
15							15
16							16
17							17
18							18
19							19
20							20
21							21
22							22
23							23
24							24
25							25
26							26
27							27
28							28
29							29
30							30
31							31
32							32
33							33
34							34

Analyze: _____

_____

PROBLEM 12.2A or 12.2B

_____

_____

_____

	ACCOUNT NAME	TRIAL BALANCE		ADJUSTMENTS	
		DEBIT	CREDIT	DEBIT	CREDIT
1					
2					
3					
4					
5					
6					
7					
8					
9					
10					
11					
12					
13					
14					
15					
16					
17					
18					
19					
20					
21					
22					
23					
24					
25					
26					
27					
28					
29					
30					
31					
32					

PROBLEM 12.2A or 12.2B (continued)

_____

_____

_____

	ADJUSTED TRIAL BALANCE			INCOME STATEMENT			BALANCE SHEET			
	DEBIT	CREDIT		DEBIT	CREDIT		DEBIT	CREDIT		
										1
										2
										3
										4
										5
										6
										7
										8
										9
										10
										11
										12
										13
										14
										15
										16
										17
										18
										19
										20
										21
										22
										23
										24
										25
										26
										27
										28
										29
										30
										31
										32

Analyze: _____

_____

PROBLEM 12.3A or 12.3B

_____

_____

	ACCOUNT NAME	TRIAL BALANCE		ADJUSTMENTS	
		DEBIT	CREDIT	DEBIT	CREDIT
1					
2					
3					
4					
5					
6					
7					
8					
9					
10					
11					
12					
13					
14					
15					
16					
17					
18					
19					
20					
21					
22					
23					
24					
25					
26					
27					
28					
29					
30					
31					
32					
33					
34					

PROBLEM 12.3A or 12.3B (continued)

	ADJUSTED TRIAL BALANCE			INCOME STATEMENT			BALANCE SHEET			
	DEBIT	CREDIT		DEBIT	CREDIT		DEBIT	CREDIT		
										1
										2
										3
										4
										5
										6
										7
										8
										9
										10
										11
										12
										13
										14
										15
										16
										17
										18
										19
										20
										21
										22
										23
										24
										25
										26
										27
										28
										29
										30
										31
										32
										33
										34

PROBLEM 12.3A or 12.3B (continued)

_____

_____

	ACCOUNT NAME	TRIAL BALANCE		ADJUSTMENTS	
		DEBIT	CREDIT	DEBIT	CREDIT
1					
2					
3					
4					
5					
6					
7					
8					
9					
10					
11					
12					
13					
14					
15					
16					
17					
18					
19					
20					
21					
22					
23					
24					
25					
26					
27					
28					
29					
30					
31					
32					

Name _____

PROBLEM 12.3A or 12.3B (continued)

ADJUSTED TRIAL BALANCE		INCOME STATEMENT		BALANCE SHEET		
DEBIT	CREDIT	DEBIT	CREDIT	DEBIT	CREDIT	
						1
						2
						3
						4
						5
						6
						7
						8
						9
						10
						11
						12
						13
						14
						15
						16
						17
						18
						19
						20
						21
						22
						23
						24
						25
						26
						27
						28
						29
						30
						31
						32

Analyze: _____

PROBLEM 12.4A or 12.4B

	ACCOUNT NAME	TRIAL BALANCE		ADJUSTMENTS	
		DEBIT	CREDIT	DEBIT	CREDIT
1					
2					
3					
4					
5					
6					
7					
8					
9					
10					
11					
12					
13					
14					
15					
16					
17					
18					
19					
20					
21					
22					
23					
24					
25					
26					
27					
28					
29					
30					
31					
32					
33					
34					

PROBLEM 12.4A or 12.4B (continued)

ADJUSTED TRIAL BALANCE		INCOME STATEMENT		BALANCE SHEET		
DEBIT	CREDIT	DEBIT	CREDIT	DEBIT	CREDIT	
						1
						2
						3
						4
						5
						6
						7
						8
						9
						10
						11
						12
						13
						14
						15
						16
						17
						18
						19
						20
						21
						22
						23
						24
						25
						26
						27
						28
						29
						30
						31
						32
						33
						34

PROBLEM 12.4A or 12.4B (continued)

	ACCOUNT NAME	TRIAL BALANCE		ADJUSTMENTS	
		DEBIT	CREDIT	DEBIT	CREDIT
1					
2					
3					
4					
5					
6					
7					
8					
9					
10					
11					
12					
13					
14					
15					
16					
17					
18					
19					
20					
21					
22					
23					
24					
25					
26					
27					
28					
29					
30					
31					
32					

PROBLEM 12.4A or 12.4B (continued)

ADJUSTED TRIAL BALANCE		INCOME STATEMENT		BALANCE SHEET		
DEBIT	CREDIT	DEBIT	CREDIT	DEBIT	CREDIT	
						1
						2
						3
						4
						5
						6
						7
						8
						9
						10
						11
						12
						13
						14
						15
						16
						17
						18
						19
						20
						21
						22
						23
						24
						25
						26
						27
						28
						29
						30
						31
						32

Analyze: _____

_____

CHAPTER 12 CHALLENGE PROBLEM

_____

_____

	ACCOUNT NAME	TRIAL BALANCE		ADJUSTMENTS	
		DEBIT	CREDIT	DEBIT	CREDIT
1					
2					
3					
4					
5					
6					
7					
8					
9					
10					
11					
12					
13					
14					
15					
16					
17					
18					
19					
20					
21					
22					
23					
24					
25					
26					
27					
28					
29					
30					
31					
32					
33					

CHAPTER 12 CHALLENGE PROBLEM (continued)

ADJUSTED TRIAL BALANCE		INCOME STATEMENT		BALANCE SHEET		
DEBIT	CREDIT	DEBIT	CREDIT	DEBIT	CREDIT	
						1
						2
						3
						4
						5
						6
						7
						8
						9
						10
						11
						12
						13
						14
						15
						16
						17
						18
						19
						20
						21
						22
						23
						24
						25
						26
						27
						28
						29
						30
						31
						32
						33

CHAPTER 12 CHALLENGE PROBLEM (continued)

	ACCOUNT NAME	TRIAL BALANCE		ADJUSTMENTS	
		DEBIT	CREDIT	DEBIT	CREDIT
1					
2					
3					
4					
5					
6					
7					
8					
9					
10					
11					
12					
13					
14					
15					
16					
17					
18					
19					
20					
21					
22					
23					
24					
25					
26					
27					
28					
29					
30					
31					
32					

CHAPTER 12 CHALLENGE PROBLEM (continued)

	ADJUSTED TRIAL BALANCE		INCOME STATEMENT		BALANCE SHEET		
	DEBIT	CREDIT	DEBIT	CREDIT	DEBIT	CREDIT	
							1
							2
							3
							4
							5
							6
							7
							8
							9
							10
							11
							12
							13
							14
							15
							16
							17
							18
							19
							20
							21
							22
							23
							24
							25
							26
							27
							28
							29
							30
							31
							32

CHAPTER 12 CHALLENGE PROBLEM (continued)

GENERAL JOURNAL

PAGE ___30___

	DATE	DESCRIPTION	POST. REF.	DEBIT	CREDIT	
1						1
2						2
3						3
4						4
5						5
6						6
7						7
8						8
9						9
10						10
11						11
12						12
13						13
14						14
15						15
16						16
17						17
18						18
19						19
20						20
21						21
22						22
23						23
24						24
25						25
26						26
27						27
28						28
29						29
30						30
31						31
32						32
33						33
34						34
35						35
36						36
37						37

CHAPTER 12 CHALLENGE PROBLEM (continued)

GENERAL JOURNAL

	DATE	DESCRIPTION	POST. REF.	DEBIT	CREDIT	
1						1
2						2
3						3
4						4
5						5
6						6
7						7
8						8
9						9
10						10
11						11
12						12
13						13
14						14
15						15
16						16
17						17
18						18
19						19
20						20
21						21
22						22
23						23
24						24
25						25
26						26
27						27
28						28
29						29
30						30
31						31
32						32
33						33
34						34
35						35
36						36
37						37

CHAPTER 12 CHALLENGE PROBLEM (continued)

a. Net Sales _____

_____

_____

b. Net Delivered
Cost of Purchases _____

_____

_____

_____

_____

c. Cost of Goods Sold _____

_____

_____

_____

d. Net Income _____

e. Capital _____

_____

_____

_____

Analyze: _____

CHAPTER 12 CRITICAL THINKING PROBLEM

1. _____
_____
_____
_____

2. _____
_____
_____
_____
_____
_____
_____
_____
_____
_____
_____
_____
_____
_____
_____
_____
_____
_____
_____
_____
_____
_____

Name _____

Chapter 12 Practice Test Answer Key

Part A True-False

1. F		14. F	
2. T		15. T	
3. F		16. F	
4. T		17. F	
5. T		18. T	
6. F		19. T	
7. F		20. T	
8. T		21. T	
9. T		22. T	
10. T		23. F	
11. F		24. F	
12. T		25. T	
13. T			

Part B Exercises

2007	(Adjustment 1)		
Dec. 31	Supplies Expense	1,000.00	
	Store Supplies		1,000.00
	(Adjustment 2)		
31	Interest Expense	20.00	
	Interest Payable		20.00
	(Adjustment 3)		
31	Interest Receivable	30.00	
	Interest Income		30.00
	(Adjustment 4)		
31	Insurance Expense	380.00	
	Prepaid Insurance		380.00

CHAPTER 13

Financial Statements and Closing Procedures

STUDY GUIDE

Understanding the Chapter

Objectives

1. Prepare a classified income statement from the worksheet. 2. Prepare a statement of owner's equity from the worksheet. 3. Prepare a classified balance sheet from the worksheet. 4. Journalize and post the adjusting entries. 5. Journalize and post the closing entries. 6. Prepare a postclosing trial balance. 7. Journalize and post reversing entries. 8. Define the accounting terms new to this chapter.

Reading Assignment

Read Chapter 13 in the textbook. Complete the textbook Section Self Review as you finish reading each section of the chapter, and the Comprehensive Self Review at the end of the chapter. Refer to the Chapter 13 Glossary or to the Glossary at the end of the book to find definitions for terms that are not familiar to you.

Activities

❏ **Thinking Critically** Answer the *Thinking Critically* questions for Safeway Inc., Computers in Accounting, and Managerial Implications.

❏ **Internet Applications** Complete the activity for Computers in Accounting.

❏ **Discussion Questions** Answer each assigned discussion question in Chapter 13.

❏ **Exercises** Complete each assigned exercise in Chapter 13. Use the forms provided in this SGWP. The objectives covered by an exercise are given after the exercise number. If you need help with an exercise, review the portion of the chapter related to the objective(s) covered.

❏ **Problems A/B** Complete each assigned problem in Chapter 13. Use the forms provided in this SGWP. The objectives covered by a problem are given after the problem number. If you need help with a problem review the portion of the chapter related to the objective(s) covered.

❏ **Challenge Problem** Complete the challenge problem as assigned. Use the forms provided in this SGWP.

❏ **Critical Thinking Problem** Complete the critical thinking problem as assigned. Use the forms provided in this SGWP.

❏ **Business Connections** Complete the Business Connections activities as assigned to gain a deeper understanding of Chapter 13 concepts.

Practice Tests

Complete the Practice Tests, which cover the main points in your reading assignment. Compare your answers with those in the Practice Test Answer Key for Chapter 13 at the end of this chapter. If you have answered any questions incorrectly, review the related section of text.

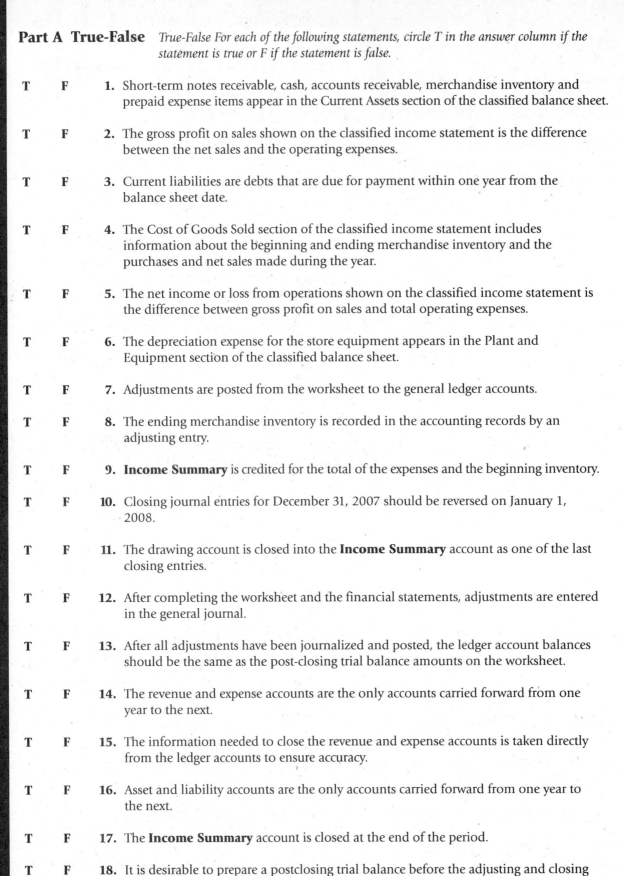

Part A True-False *True-False For each of the following statements, circle T in the answer column if the statement is true or F if the statement is false.*

T   F   **1.** Short-term notes receivable, cash, accounts receivable, merchandise inventory and prepaid expense items appear in the Current Assets section of the classified balance sheet.

T   F   **2.** The gross profit on sales shown on the classified income statement is the difference between the net sales and the operating expenses.

T   F   **3.** Current liabilities are debts that are due for payment within one year from the balance sheet date.

T   F   **4.** The Cost of Goods Sold section of the classified income statement includes information about the beginning and ending merchandise inventory and the purchases and net sales made during the year.

T   F   **5.** The net income or loss from operations shown on the classified income statement is the difference between gross profit on sales and total operating expenses.

T   F   **6.** The depreciation expense for the store equipment appears in the Plant and Equipment section of the classified balance sheet.

T   F   **7.** Adjustments are posted from the worksheet to the general ledger accounts.

T   F   **8.** The ending merchandise inventory is recorded in the accounting records by an adjusting entry.

T   F   **9. Income Summary** is credited for the total of the expenses and the beginning inventory.

T   F   **10.** Closing journal entries for December 31, 2007 should be reversed on January 1, 2008.

T   F   **11.** The drawing account is closed into the **Income Summary** account as one of the last closing entries.

T   F   **12.** After completing the worksheet and the financial statements, adjustments are entered in the general journal.

T   F   **13.** After all adjustments have been journalized and posted, the ledger account balances should be the same as the post-closing trial balance amounts on the worksheet.

T   F   **14.** The revenue and expense accounts are the only accounts carried forward from one year to the next.

T   F   **15.** The information needed to close the revenue and expense accounts is taken directly from the ledger accounts to ensure accuracy.

T   F   **16.** Asset and liability accounts are the only accounts carried forward from one year to the next.

T   F   **17.** The **Income Summary** account is closed at the end of the period.

T   F   **18.** It is desirable to prepare a postclosing trial balance before the adjusting and closing entries have been journalized and posted.

T   F   **19.** The postclosing trial balance shows essentially the same account balances that appear in the balance sheet.

T   F   **20.** In closing the **Income Summary** account, the net income or loss is closed into the owner's capital account.

T   F   **21.** Reversing entries are not required, but are highly recommended in order to improve efficiency and reduce errors.

T   F   **22.** The information found in the Statement of Owner's Equity may be shown in the balance sheet instead of on a separate statement.

T   F   **23.** Some accounts adjusted in the Adjustment columns of the worksheet do not require a reversing entry.

T   F   **24.** **Accrued Interest on Notes Payable** and **Depreciation Expense** are typical of accounts that do not require reversing entries.

T   F   **25.** If an adjusting entry opens a new asset or liability account, the entry will probably be reversed.

Demonstration Problem

A partial worksheet showing the end-of-year operating results for Super Sports for 2007 follows.

Instructions

1. Prepare a classified income statement. Super Sports does not classify its operating expenses as selling and administrative expenses.

2. Prepare a statement of owner's equity. No additional investments were made during the period.

3. Prepare a classified balance sheet as of December 31, 2007. All notes payable are due within one year.

4. Journalize the closing entries on page 45 of the general journal.

Super Sports

Worksheet (Partial)

Year Ended December 31, 2007

	ACCOUNT NAME	INCOME STATEMENT DEBIT	INCOME STATEMENT CREDIT	BALANCE SHEET DEBIT	BALANCE SHEET CREDIT
1	Cash			17 2 8 5 00	
2	Accounts Receivable			56 2 5 8 00	
3	Allowance for Doubtful Accounts				5 8 4 0 00
4	Merchandise Inventory			197 2 1 4 00	
5	Supplies			3 6 1 2 00	
6	Prepaid Insurance			3 7 0 0 0 00	
7	Equipment			83 2 9 0 00	
8	Accumulated Depreciation—Equipment				24 3 3 0 00
9	Notes Payable				47 5 0 0 00
10	Accounts Payable				42 8 6 0 00
11	Social Security Tax Payable				2 6 8 3 00
12	Medicare Tax Payable				8 4 5 00
13	Salaries Payable				6 5 3 0 00
14	Interest Payable				3 6 6 0 00
15	Nau Flores, Capital				260 7 3 0 00
16	Nau Flores, Drawing			50 0 0 0 00	
17	Income Summary	201 3 4 5 00	197 2 1 4 00		
18	Sales		610 6 9 0 00		
19	Sales Returns and Allowances	11 9 5 0 00			
20	Purchases	277 1 7 4 00			
21	Purchases Returns and Allowances		10 4 4 0 00		
22	Freight In	11 4 1 0 00			
23	Purchases Discounts		11 9 2 1 00		
24	Telephone Expense	3 1 7 1 00			
25	Salaries Expense	240 3 8 0 00			
26	Payroll Tax Expense	13 1 0 4 00			
27	Supplies Expense	5 9 6 0 00			
28	Insurance Expense	4 0 0 0 00			
29	Depreciation Expense—Equipment	7 4 2 0 00			
30	Uncollectible Accounts Expense	2 5 1 0 00			
31	Interest Expense	2 1 6 0 00			
32	Totals	780 5 8 4 00	830 2 6 5 00	444 6 5 9 00	394 9 7 8 00
33	Net Income	49 6 8 1 00			49 6 8 1 00
34		830 2 6 5 00	830 2 6 5 00	444 6 5 9 00	444 6 5 9 00
35					

SOLUTION

Super Sports
Income Statement
Year Ended December 31, 2007

Operating Revenue				
Sales				610 6 9 0 00
Less Sales Returns and Allowances				11 9 5 0 00
Net Sales				598 7 4 0 00
Cost of Goods Sold				
Merchandise Inventory, Jan. 1, 2007			201 3 4 5 00	
Purchases		277 1 7 4 00		
Freight In		11 4 1 0 00		
Delivered Cost of Purchases		288 5 8 4 00		
Less Purchase Returns and Allow.	10 4 4 0 00			
Purchase Discounts	11 9 2 1 00	22 3 6 1 00		
Net Delivered Cost of Purchases			266 2 2 3 00	
Total Merchandise Available for Sale			467 5 6 8 00	
Less Merchandise Inv., Dec. 31, 2007			197 2 1 4 00	
Cost of Goods Sold				270 3 5 4 00
Gross Profit on Sales				328 3 8 6 00
Operating Expenses				
Telephone Expense			3 1 7 1 00	
Salaries Expense			240 3 8 0 00	
Payroll Tax Expense			13 1 0 4 00	
Supplies Expense			5 9 6 0 00	
Insurance Expense			4 0 0 0 00	
Depreciation Expense—Equipment			7 4 2 0 00	
Uncollectible Accounts Expense			2 5 1 0 00	
Total Operating Expenses				276 5 4 5 00
Income from Operations				51 8 4 1 00
Other Expenses				
Interest Expense				2 1 6 0 00
Net Income for Year				49 6 8 1 00

SOLUTION (continued)

Super Sports

Statement of Owner's Equity

Year Ended December 31, 2007

Nau Flores, Capital, Jan. 1, 2007			260 7 3 0 00
Net Income for Year		49 6 8 1 00	
Less Withdrawals for the Year		50 0 0 0 00	
Increase in Capital			− 3 1 9 00
Nau Flores, Capital, Dec. 31, 2007			260 4 1 1 00

Super Sports

Balance Sheet

December 31, 2007

Assets			
Current Assets			
Cash			17 2 8 5 00
Accounts Receivable		56 2 5 8 00	
Less Allowance for Doubtful Accounts		5 8 4 0 00	50 4 1 8 00
Merchandise Inventory			197 2 1 4 00
Prepaid Expenses			
Supplies		3 6 1 2 00	
Prepaid Insurance		37 0 0 0 00	40 6 1 2 00
Total Current Assets			305 5 2 9 00
Plant and Equipment			
Equipment	83 2 9 0 00		
Less Accumulated Depreciation	24 3 3 0 00	58 9 6 0 00	
Total Plant and Equipment			58 9 6 0 00
Total Assets			364 4 8 9 00
Liabilities and Owner's Equity			
Current Liabilities			
Notes Payable		47 5 0 0 00	
Accounts Payable		42 8 6 0 00	
Interest Payable		3 6 6 0 00	
Social Security Tax Payable		2 6 8 3 00	
Medicare Tax Payable		8 4 5 00	
Salaries Payable		6 5 3 0 00	
Total Current Liabilities			104 0 7 8 00
Owner's Equity			
Nau Flores, Capital			260 4 1 1 00
Total Liabilities and Owner's Equity			364 4 8 9 00

SOLUTION (continued)

GENERAL JOURNAL   PAGE ___45___

	DATE		DESCRIPTION	POST. REF.	DEBIT	CREDIT	
1			**Closing Entries**				1
2	**2007**						2
3	Dec.	31	**Sales**		610 6 9 0 00		3
4			**Purchase Returns and Allowances**		10 4 4 0 00		4
5			**Purchases Discounts**		11 9 2 1 00		5
6			**Income Summary**			633 0 5 1 00	6
7							7
8		31	**Income Summary**		579 2 3 9 00		8
9			**Sales Returns and Allowances**			11 9 5 0 00	9
10			**Purchases**			277 1 7 4 00	10
11			**Freight In**			11 4 1 0 00	11
12			**Telephone Expense**			3 1 7 1 00	12
13			**Salaries Expense**			240 3 8 0 00	13
14			**Payroll Taxes Expense**			13 1 0 4 00	14
15			**Supplies Expense**			5 9 6 0 00	15
16			**Insurance Expense**			4 0 0 0 00	16
17			**Depreciation Expense—Equipment**			7 4 2 0 00	17
18			**Uncollectible Accounts Expense**			2 5 1 0 00	18
19			**Interest Expense**			2 1 6 0 00	19
20							20
21		31	**Income Summary**		49 6 8 1 00		21
22			**Nau Flores, Capital**			49 6 8 1 00	22
23							23
24		31	**Nau Flores, Capital**		50 0 0 0 00		24
25			**Nau Flores, Drawing**			50 0 0 0 00	25
26							26
27							27
28							28
29							29
30							30
31							31
32							32
33							33
34							34
35							35
36							36

WORKING PAPERS

Name _____

EXERCISE 13.1

1. Rent Expense _____

2. Depreciation Expense—
   Store Equipment _____

3. Sales _____

4. Interest Expense _____

5. Merchandise Inventory _____

6. Interest Income _____

7. Purchases _____

8. Sales Returns and Allowances _____

9. Utilities Expense _____

10. Purchase Returns
    and Allowances _____

EXERCISE 13.2

1. Rent Payable _____

2. Cash _____

3. Raja Julia, Capital _____

4. Merchandise Inventory _____

5. Accounts Payable _____

6. Store Supplies _____

7. Sales Tax Payable _____

8. Prepaid Insurance _____

9. Delivery Van _____

10. Accounts Receivable _____

EXERCISE 13.3

(continued)

EXERCISE 13.3 (continued)

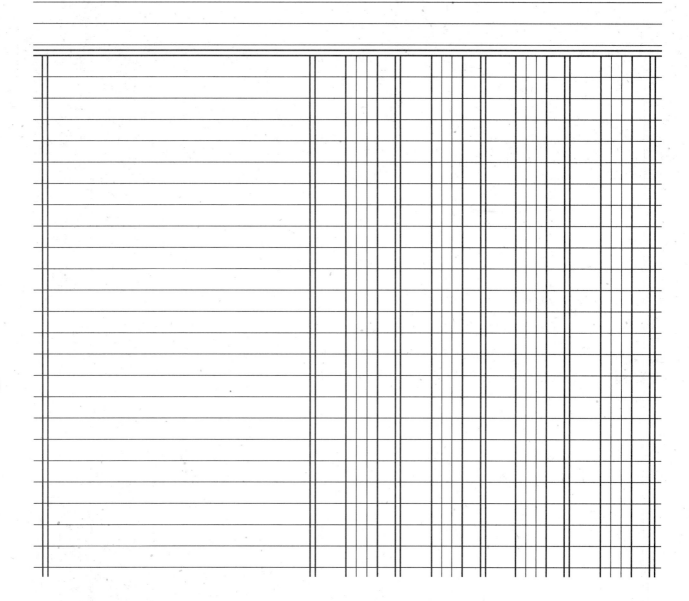

EXERCISE 13.4

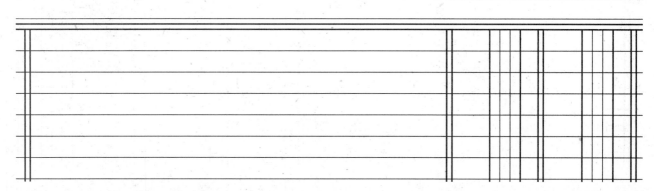

EXERCISE 13.5

EXERCISE 13.6

GENERAL JOURNAL   PAGE _____

	DATE		DESCRIPTION	POST. REF.	DEBIT	CREDIT	
1							1
2							2
3							3
4							4
5							5
6							6
7							7
8							8
9							9
10							10
11							11
12							12
13							13
14							14
15							15
16							16
17							17
18							18
19							19
20							20
21							21
22							22
23							23
24							24
25							25
26							26
27							27
28							28
29							29
30							30
31							31
32							32
33							33
34							34
35							35
36							36
37							37

EXERCISE 13.7

GENERAL JOURNAL   PAGE ___1___

	DATE		DESCRIPTION	POST. REF.	DEBIT	CREDIT	
1							1
2							2
3							3
4							4
5							5
6							6
7							7
8							8
9							9
10							10
11							11
12							12
13							13
14							14
15							15
16							16
17							17
18							18
19							19
20							20
21							21
22							22
23							23
24							24
25							25
26							26
27							27
28							28
29							29
30							30
31							31
32							32
33							33
34							34
35							35
36							36
37							37

PROBLEM 13.1A or 13.1B (continued)

Analyze: _____

PROBLEM 13.2A or 13.2B

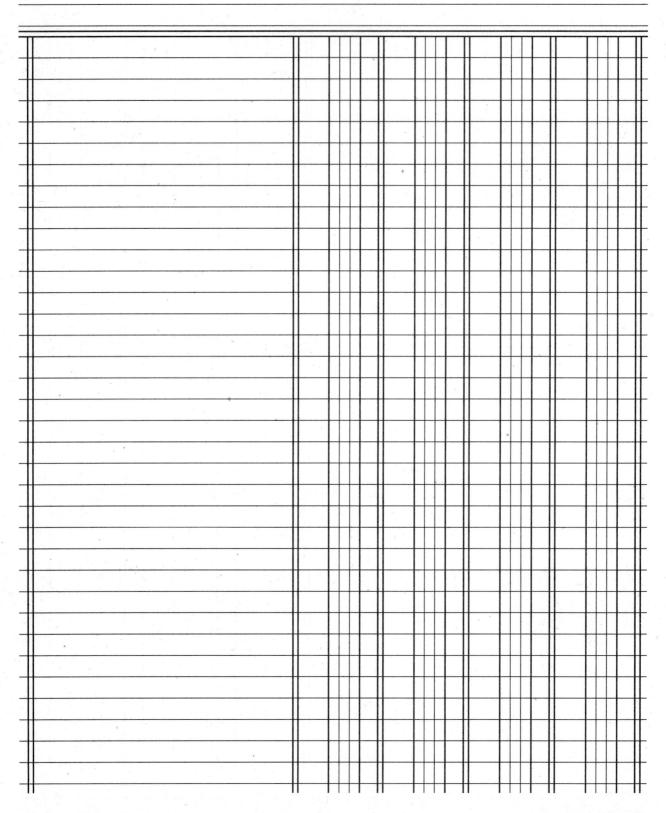

(continued)

Name _____

PROBLEM 13.2A or 13.2B (continued)

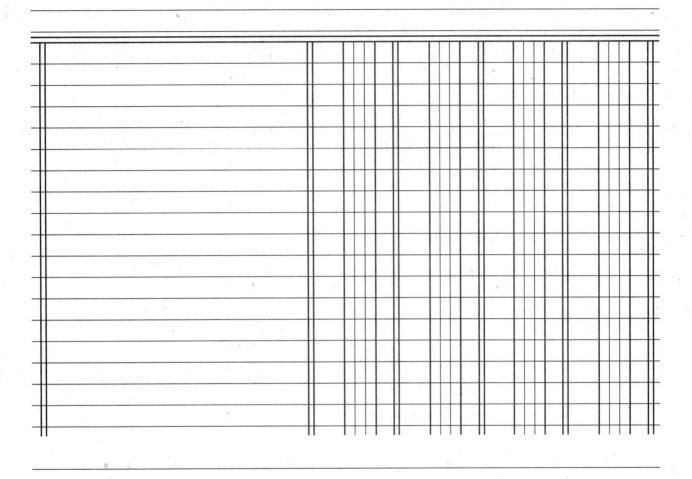

PROBLEM 13.2A or 13.2B (continued)

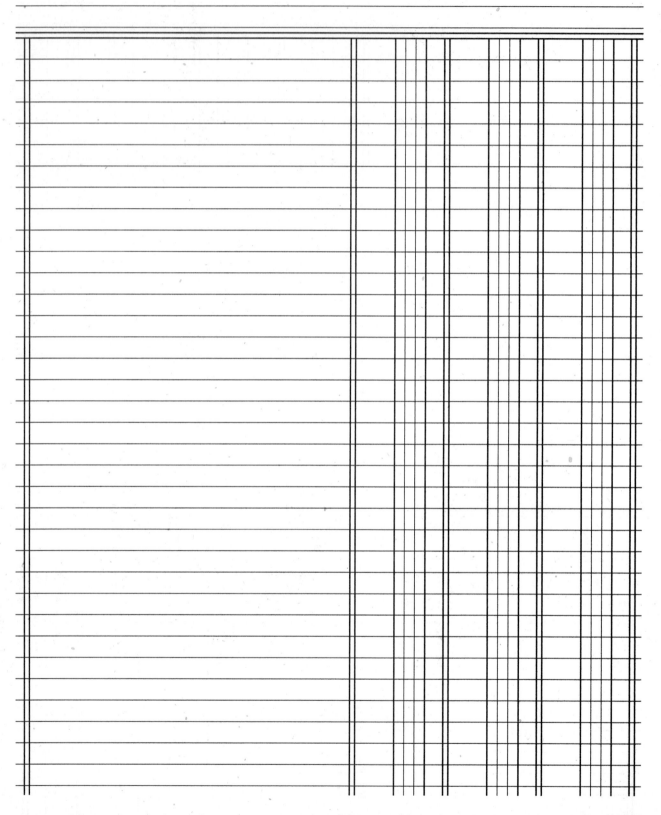

(continued)

PROBLEM 13.2A or 13.2B (continued)

Analyze: _____

_____

PROBLEM 13.3A or 13.3B

GENERAL JOURNAL   PAGE _____

	DATE		DESCRIPTION	POST. REF.	DEBIT	CREDIT	
1							1
2							2
3							3
4							4
5							5
6							6
7							7
8							8
9							9
10							10
11							11
12							12
13							13
14							14
15							15
16							16
17							17
18							18
19							19
20							20
21							21
22							22
23							23
24							24
25							25
26							26
27							27
28							28
29							29
30							30
31							31
32							32
33							33
34							34
35							35
36							36
37							37

PROBLEM 13.3A or 13.3B (continued)

GENERAL JOURNAL   PAGE _____

	DATE		DESCRIPTION	POST. REF.	DEBIT	CREDIT	
1							1
2							2
3							3
4							4
5							5
6							6
7							7
8							8
9							9
10							10
11							11
12							12
13							13
14							14
15							15
16							16
17							17
18							18
19							19
20							20
21							21
22							22
23							23
24							24
25							25
26							26
27							27
28							28
29							29
30							30
31							31
32							32
33							33
34							34
35							35
36							36
37							37

PROBLEM 13.3A or 13.3B (continued)

GENERAL JOURNAL   PAGE _____

	DATE	DESCRIPTION	POST. REF.	DEBIT	CREDIT	
1						1
2						2
3						3
4						4
5						5
6						6
7						7
8						8
9						9
10						10
11						11
12						12
13						13
14						14
15						15
16						16
17						17
18						18
19						19
20						20
21						21
22						22
23						23
24						24
25						25
26						26
27						27
28						28
29						29
30						30
31						31
32						32
33						33
34						34
35						35
36						36
37						37

PROBLEM 13.3A or 13.3B (continued)

GENERAL JOURNAL   PAGE _____

	DATE		DESCRIPTION	POST. REF.	DEBIT	CREDIT	
1							1
2							2
3							3
4							4
5							5
6							6
7							7
8							8
9							9
10							10
11							11
12							12
13							13
14							14
15							15
16							16
17							17
18							18
19							19
20							20
21							21
22							22
23							23
24							24
25							25
26							26
27							27
28							28
29							29
30							30
31							31
32							32
33							33
34							34

Analyze: _____

_____

PROBLEM 13.4A or 13.4B

GENERAL JOURNAL   PAGE _____

	DATE	DESCRIPTION	POST. REF.	DEBIT	CREDIT	
1						1
2						2
3						3
4						4
5						5
6						6
7						7
8						8
9						9
10						10
11						11
12						12
13						13
14						14
15						15
16						16
17						17
18						18
19						19
20						20
21						21
22						22
23						23
24						24
25						25
26						26
27						27
28						28
29						29
30						30
31						31
32						32
33						33
34						34
35						35
36						36

Name _____

PROBLEM 13.4A or 13.4B (continued)

GENERAL JOURNAL PAGE ___

	DATE	DESCRIPTION	POST. REF.	DEBIT	CREDIT	
1						1
2						2
3						3
4						4
5						5
6						6
7						7
8						8
9						9
10						10
11						11
12						12
13						13
14						14
15						15
16						16

Analyze: _____

EXTRA FORM

GENERAL JOURNAL PAGE ___

	DATE	DESCRIPTION	POST. REF.	DEBIT	CREDIT	
1						1
2						2
3						3
4						4
5						5
6						6
7						7
8						8
9						9
10						10
11						11
12						12
13						13

CHAPTER 13 CHALLENGE PROBLEM

	ACCOUNT NAME	TRIAL BALANCE		ADJUSTMENTS	
		DEBIT	CREDIT	DEBIT	CREDIT
1					
2					
3					
4					
5					
6					
7					
8					
9					
10					
11					
12					
13					
14					
15					
16					
17					
18					
19					
20					
21					
22					
23					
24					
25					
26					
27					
28					
29					
30					
31					
32					
33					
34					
35					
36					

CHAPTER 13 CHALLENGE PROBLEM (continued)

ADJUSTED TRIAL BALANCE		INCOME STATEMENT		BALANCE SHEET		
DEBIT	CREDIT	DEBIT	CREDIT	DEBIT	CREDIT	
						1
						2
						3
						4
						5
						6
						7
						8
						9
						10
						11
						12
						13
						14
						15
						16
						17
						18
						19
						20
						21
						22
						23
						24
						25
						26
						27
						28
						29
						30
						31
						32
						33
						34
						35
						36

Name _____

CHAPTER 13 CHALLENGE PROBLEM (continued)

EXTRA FORM

CHAPTER 13 CHALLENGE PROBLEM (continued)

CHAPTER 13 CHALLENGE PROBLEM (continued)

GENERAL JOURNAL   PAGE _____

	DATE	DESCRIPTION	POST. REF.	DEBIT	CREDIT	
1						1
2						2
3						3
4						4
5						5
6						6
7						7
8						8
9						9
10						10
11						11
12						12
13						13
14						14
15						15
16						16
17						17
18						18
19						19
20						20
21						21
22						22
23						23
24						24
25						25
26						26
27						27
28						28
29						29
30						30
31						31
32						32
33						33
34						34
35						35
36						36
37						37

CHAPTER 13 CHALLENGE PROBLEM (continued)

GENERAL JOURNAL   PAGE _____

	DATE	DESCRIPTION	POST. REF.	DEBIT	CREDIT	
1						1
2						2
3						3
4						4
5						5
6						6
7						7
8						8
9						9
10						10
11						11
12						12
13						13
14						14
15						15
16						16
17						17
18						18
19						19
20						20
21						21
22						22
23						23
24						24
25						25
26						26
27						27
28						28
29						29
30						30
31						31
32						32
33						33
34						34
35						35
36						36
37						37

CHAPTER 13 CHALLENGE PROBLEM (continued)

GENERAL JOURNAL

	DATE	DESCRIPTION	POST. REF.	DEBIT	CREDIT	
1						1
2						2
3						3
4						4
5						5
6						6
7						7
8						8
9						9
10						10
11						11
12						12
13						13
14						14
15						15
16						16
17						17
18						18
19						19
20						20
21						21
22						22
23						23
24						24
25						25
26						26
27						27
28						28
29						29
30						30
31						31
32						32
33						33
34						34
35						35
36						36
37						37

CHAPTER 13 CHALLENGE PROBLEM (continued)

GENERAL JOURNAL   PAGE _____

	DATE		DESCRIPTION	POST. REF.	DEBIT	CREDIT	
1							1
2							2
3							3
4							4
5							5
6							6
7							7
8							8
9							9
10							10
11							11
12							12
13							13
14							14
15							15
16							16
17							17
18							18
19							19
20							20
21							21
22							22
23							23
24							24
25							25
26							26
27							27
28							28
29							29
30							30
31							31
32							32
33							33
34							34

Analyze: _____

_____

CHAPTER 13 CRITICAL THINKING PROBLEM

1.

_____
_____

2. _____
_____
_____
_____
_____
_____
_____

CHAPTER 13 CRITICAL THINKING PROBLEM (continued)

3. _____

Chapter 13 Practice Test Answer Key

Part A True-False

1. T	6. F	11. F	16. F	21. T
2. F	7. F	12. T	17. T	22. T
3. T	8. T	13. F	18. F	23. T
4. F	9. F	14. F	19. T	24. F
5. T	10. F	15. F	20. T	25. T

MINI-PRACTICE SET 2

Merchandising Business Accounting Cycle

SALES JOURNAL

PAGE _____

	DATE		SALES SLIP NO.	CUSTOMER'S NAME	POST. REF.	ACCOUNTS RECEIVABLE DEBIT	SALES TAX PAYABLE CREDIT	SALES CREDIT	
1									1
2									2
3									3
4									4
5									5
6									6
7									7
8									8
9									9
10									10
11									11
12									12
13									13
14									14

PURCHASES JOURNAL

PAGE _____

DATE	PURCHASED FROM	INVOICE NUMBER	INVOICE DATE	TERMS	POST. REF.	PURCHASES DR./ ACCOUNTS PAYABLE CR.

Name

PAGE

CASH RECEIPTS JOURNAL

DATE	DESCRIPTION	POST. REF.	ACCOUNTS RECEIVABLE CREDIT	SALES TAX PAYABLE CREDIT	SALES CREDIT	OTHER ACCOUNTS CREDIT			CASH DEBIT
						ACCOUNT NAME	POST. REF.	AMOUNT	

CASH PAYMENTS JOURNAL

DATE	CK. NO.	DESCRIPTION	POST. REF.	ACCOUNTS PAYABLE DEBIT	OTHER ACCOUNTS DEBIT			PURCHASES DISCOUNT CREDIT	CASH CREDIT
					ACCOUNT NAME	POST. REF.	AMOUNT		

Name _____

GENERAL JOURNAL   PAGE _____

	DATE		DESCRIPTION	POST. REF.	DEBIT	CREDIT	
1							1
2							2
3							3
4							4
5							5
6							6
7							7
8							8
9							9
10							10
11							11
12							12
13							13
14							14
15							15
16							16
17							17
18							18
19							19
20							20
21							21
22							22
23							23
24							24
25							25
26							26
27							27
28							28
29							29
30							30
31							31
32							32
33							33
34							34
35							35
36							36
37							37
38							38

Name _____

GENERAL JOURNAL

PAGE _____

	DATE		DESCRIPTION	POST. REF.	DEBIT	CREDIT	
1							1
2							2
3							3
4							4
5							5
6							6
7							7
8							8
9							9
10							10
11							11
12							12
13							13
14							14
15							15
16							16
17							17
18							18
19							19
20							20
21							21
22							22
23							23
24							24
25							25
26							26
27							27
28							28
29							29
30							30
31							31
32							32
33							33
34							34
35							35
36							36
37							37
38							38

Name _____

GENERAL JOURNAL

PAGE _____

	DATE		DESCRIPTION	POST. REF.	DEBIT	CREDIT	
1							1
2							2
3							3
4							4
5							5
6							6
7							7
8							8
9							9
10							10
11							11
12							12
13							13
14							14
15							15
16							16
17							17
18							18
19							19
20							20
21							21
22							22
23							23
24							24
25							25
26							26
27							27
28							28
29							29
30							30
31							31
32							32
33							33
34							34
35							35
36							36
37							37
38							38

GENERAL LEDGER

ACCOUNT _____   ACCOUNT NO. _____

DATE	DESCRIPTION	POST. REF.	DEBIT	CREDIT	BALANCE	
					DEBIT	CREDIT

ACCOUNT _____   ACCOUNT NO. _____

DATE	DESCRIPTION	POST. REF.	DEBIT	CREDIT	BALANCE	
					DEBIT	CREDIT

ACCOUNT _____   ACCOUNT NO. _____

DATE	DESCRIPTION	POST. REF.	DEBIT	CREDIT	BALANCE	
					DEBIT	CREDIT

ACCOUNT _____   ACCOUNT NO. _____

DATE	DESCRIPTION	POST. REF.	DEBIT	CREDIT	BALANCE	
					DEBIT	CREDIT

GENERAL LEDGER

ACCOUNT _____ ACCOUNT NO. _____

DATE	DESCRIPTION	POST. REF.	DEBIT	CREDIT	BALANCE	
					DEBIT	CREDIT

ACCOUNT _____ ACCOUNT NO. _____

DATE	DESCRIPTION	POST. REF.	DEBIT	CREDIT	BALANCE	
					DEBIT	CREDIT

ACCOUNT _____ ACCOUNT NO. _____

DATE	DESCRIPTION	POST. REF.	DEBIT	CREDIT	BALANCE	
					DEBIT	CREDIT

ACCOUNT _____ ACCOUNT NO. _____

DATE	DESCRIPTION	POST. REF.	DEBIT	CREDIT	BALANCE	
					DEBIT	CREDIT

ACCOUNT _____ ACCOUNT NO. _____

DATE	DESCRIPTION	POST. REF.	DEBIT	CREDIT	BALANCE	
					DEBIT	CREDIT

GENERAL LEDGER

ACCOUNT _____   ACCOUNT NO. _____

DATE	DESCRIPTION	POST. REF.	DEBIT	CREDIT	BALANCE	
					DEBIT	CREDIT

ACCOUNT _____   ACCOUNT NO. _____

DATE	DESCRIPTION	POST. REF.	DEBIT	CREDIT	BALANCE	
					DEBIT	CREDIT

ACCOUNT _____   ACCOUNT NO. _____

DATE	DESCRIPTION	POST. REF.	DEBIT	CREDIT	BALANCE	
					DEBIT	CREDIT

ACCOUNT _____   ACCOUNT NO. _____

DATE	DESCRIPTION	POST. REF.	DEBIT	CREDIT	BALANCE	
					DEBIT	CREDIT

Name _____

GENERAL LEDGER

ACCOUNT _____ ACCOUNT NO. _____

DATE	DESCRIPTION	POST. REF.	DEBIT	CREDIT	BALANCE	
					DEBIT	CREDIT

ACCOUNT _____ ACCOUNT NO. _____

DATE	DESCRIPTION	POST. REF.	DEBIT	CREDIT	BALANCE	
					DEBIT	CREDIT

ACCOUNT _____ ACCOUNT NO. _____

DATE	DESCRIPTION	POST. REF.	DEBIT	CREDIT	BALANCE	
					DEBIT	CREDIT

ACCOUNT _____ ACCOUNT NO. _____

DATE	DESCRIPTION	POST. REF.	DEBIT	CREDIT	BALANCE	
					DEBIT	CREDIT

ACCOUNT _____ ACCOUNT NO. _____

DATE	DESCRIPTION	POST. REF.	DEBIT	CREDIT	BALANCE	
					DEBIT	CREDIT

GENERAL LEDGER

ACCOUNT _____ ACCOUNT NO. _____

DATE	DESCRIPTION	POST. REF.	DEBIT	CREDIT	BALANCE	
					DEBIT	CREDIT

ACCOUNT _____ ACCOUNT NO. _____

DATE	DESCRIPTION	POST. REF.	DEBIT	CREDIT	BALANCE	
					DEBIT	CREDIT

ACCOUNT _____ ACCOUNT NO. _____

DATE	DESCRIPTION	POST. REF.	DEBIT	CREDIT	BALANCE	
					DEBIT	CREDIT

ACCOUNT _____ ACCOUNT NO. _____

DATE	DESCRIPTION	POST. REF.	DEBIT	CREDIT	BALANCE	
					DEBIT	CREDIT

Name _____

GENERAL LEDGER

ACCOUNT _____ ACCOUNT NO. _____

DATE	DESCRIPTION	POST. REF.	DEBIT	CREDIT	BALANCE DEBIT	BALANCE CREDIT

ACCOUNT _____ ACCOUNT NO. _____

DATE	DESCRIPTION	POST. REF.	DEBIT	CREDIT	BALANCE DEBIT	BALANCE CREDIT

ACCOUNT _____ ACCOUNT NO. _____

DATE	DESCRIPTION	POST. REF.	DEBIT	CREDIT	BALANCE DEBIT	BALANCE CREDIT

ACCOUNT _____ ACCOUNT NO. _____

DATE	DESCRIPTION	POST. REF.	DEBIT	CREDIT	BALANCE DEBIT	BALANCE CREDIT

ACCOUNT _____ ACCOUNT NO. _____

DATE	DESCRIPTION	POST. REF.	DEBIT	CREDIT	BALANCE DEBIT	BALANCE CREDIT

Name _____

GENERAL LEDGER

ACCOUNT _____ ACCOUNT NO. _____

DATE	DESCRIPTION	POST. REF.	DEBIT	CREDIT	BALANCE	
					DEBIT	CREDIT

ACCOUNT _____ ACCOUNT NO. _____

DATE	DESCRIPTION	POST. REF.	DEBIT	CREDIT	BALANCE	
					DEBIT	CREDIT

ACCOUNT _____ ACCOUNT NO. _____

DATE	DESCRIPTION	POST. REF.	DEBIT	CREDIT	BALANCE	
					DEBIT	CREDIT

ACCOUNT _____ ACCOUNT NO. _____

DATE	DESCRIPTION	POST. REF.	DEBIT	CREDIT	BALANCE	
					DEBIT	CREDIT

ACCOUNT _____ ACCOUNT NO. _____

DATE	DESCRIPTION	POST. REF.	DEBIT	CREDIT	BALANCE	
					DEBIT	CREDIT

ACCOUNTS RECEIVABLE SUBSIDIARY LEDGER

NAME _____ TERMS _____

	DATE	DESCRIPTION	POST. REF.	DEBIT	CREDIT	BALANCE

NAME _____ TERMS _____

	DATE	DESCRIPTION	POST. REF.	DEBIT	CREDIT	BALANCE

NAME _____ TERMS _____

	DATE	DESCRIPTION	POST. REF.	DEBIT	CREDIT	BALANCE

NAME _____ TERMS _____

	DATE	DESCRIPTION	POST. REF.	DEBIT	CREDIT	BALANCE

NAME _____ TERMS _____

	DATE	DESCRIPTION	POST. REF.	DEBIT	CREDIT	BALANCE

ACCOUNTS RECEIVABLE SUBSIDIARY LEDGER

NAME _____   TERMS _____

	DATE	DESCRIPTION	POST. REF.	DEBIT	CREDIT	BALANCE

NAME _____   TERMS _____

	DATE	DESCRIPTION	POST. REF.	DEBIT	CREDIT	BALANCE

ACCOUNTS PAYABLE SUBSIDIARY LEDGER

NAME _____   TERMS _____

	DATE	DESCRIPTION	POST. REF.	DEBIT	CREDIT	BALANCE

NAME _____   TERMS _____

	DATE	DESCRIPTION	POST. REF.	DEBIT	CREDIT	BALANCE

ACCOUNTS PAYABLE SUBSIDIARY LEDGER

NAME _____   TERMS _____

DATE	DESCRIPTION	POST. REF.	DEBIT	CREDIT	BALANCE

DATE	DESCRIPTION	POST. REF.	DEBIT	CREDIT	BALANCE

DATE	DESCRIPTION	POST. REF.	DEBIT	CREDIT	BALANCE

	ACCOUNT NAME	TRIAL BALANCE		ADJUSTMENTS	
		DEBIT	CREDIT	DEBIT	CREDIT
1					
2					
3					
4					
5					
6					
7					
8					
9					
10					
11					
12					
13					
14					
15					
16					
17					
18					
19					
20					
21					
22					
23					
24					
25					
26					
27					
28					
29					
30					
31					
32					
33					
34					
35					
36					

ADJUSTED TRIAL BALANCE		INCOME STATEMENT		BALANCE SHEET		
DEBIT	CREDIT	DEBIT	CREDIT	DEBIT	CREDIT	
						1
						2
						3
						4
						5
						6
						7
						8
						9
						10
						11
						12
						13
						14
						15
						16
						17
						18
						19
						20
						21
						22
						23
						24
						25
						26
						27
						28
						29
						30
						31
						32
						33
						34
						35
						36

	ACCOUNT NAME	TRIAL BALANCE		ADJUSTMENTS	
		DEBIT	CREDIT	DEBIT	CREDIT
1					
2					
3					
4					
5					
6					
7					
8					
9					
10					
11					
12					
13					
14					
15					
16					
17					
18					
19					
20					
21					
22					
23					
24					
25					
26					
27					
28					
29					
30					
31					
32					
33					
34					
35					
36					

ADJUSTED TRIAL BALANCE		INCOME STATEMENT		BALANCE SHEET		
DEBIT	CREDIT	DEBIT	CREDIT	DEBIT	CREDIT	
						1
						2
						3
						4
						5
						6
						7
						8
						9
						10
						11
						12
						13
						14
						15
						16
						17
						18
						19
						20
						21
						22
						23
						24
						25
						26
						27
						28
						29
						30
						31
						32
						33
						34
						35
						36

MINI-PRACTICE SET 2 (continued)   Name _____

ACCOUNT NAME	DEBIT	CREDIT

_____

_____

_____

	ACCOUNT NAME	TRIAL BALANCE		ADJUSTMENTS	
		DEBIT	CREDIT	DEBIT	CREDIT
1					
2					
3					
4					
5					
6					
7					
8					
9					
10					
11					
12					
13					
14					
15					
16					
17					
18					
19					
20					
21					
22					
23					
24					
25					
26					
27					
28					
29					
30					
31					
32					
33					
34					

_____

_____

ADJUSTED TRIAL BALANCE		INCOME STATEMENT		BALANCE SHEET		
DEBIT	CREDIT	DEBIT	CREDIT	DEBIT	CREDIT	
						1
						2
						3
						4
						5
						6
						7
						8
						9
						10
						11
						12
						13
						14
						15
						16
						17
						18
						19
						20
						21
						22
						23
						24
						25
						26
						27
						28
						29
						30
						31
						32
						33
						34

EXTRA FORM

GENERAL JOURNAL   PAGE _____

	DATE	DESCRIPTION	POST. REF.	DEBIT	CREDIT	
1						1
2						2
3						3
4						4
5						5
6						6
7						7
8						8
9						9
10						10
11						11
12						12
13						13
14						14
15						15
16						16
17						17
18						18
19						19
20						20
21						21
22						22
23						23
24						24
25						25
26						26
27						27
28						28
29						29
30						30
31						31
32						32
33						33
34						34
35						35
36						36
37						37